MARRIAGE COMMUNICATION GUIDE FOR NEW COUPLES

FROM "ME" TO "WE": BUILDING A SHARED LANGUAGE FOR YOUR RELATIONSHIP

ERIC A. WILLIAMS, PH.D

www.TrueVinePublishing.org

Marriage Communication Guide for New Couples
Eric A. Williams, Ph.D

Published by True Vine Publishing Co.
810 Dominican Dr.
Nashville, TN 37228
www.TrueVinePublishing.org

ISBN: 978-1-962783-34-7 Paperback
ISBN: 978-1-962783-30-9 eBook

Printed in the United States of America—First printing

DEDICATION

To all the couples who have found "the one," individuals seeking that special someone, and those pondering what might be amiss in their relationships, this book is for you, inspired by others like you.

Trust me, you'll either learn the contents of this book before things get complicated or afterwards. But waiting until later will only leave you regretful that you and your partner didn't read it sooner. So, let's not delay. What you can read today, don't put off till tomorrow. Remember, caring means sharing; be sure to pass this message on to others who may benefit from it. And I'm sure you know a few such people. We all have someone in mind who could use this book. They'll thank you for it later.

ACKNOWLEDGEMENTS

The birth of my first book would not be possible without the support from a team of people in my inner circle. First and foremost, I'd like to acknowledge my loving wife, Dana Williams, for tolerating me and my poor and ineffective communication throughout our marriage. My stubbornness versus your patience and grace was an epic battle that I can truly say I'm very fortunate that I lost. And thank you for "giving me three kids" who also helped me improve my communication skills.

I want to acknowledge my mother, Freddy M. Hobbs, for inspiring me to be a reader throughout my childhood and for challenging me to expand my comfort zone which has also inspired me to write. Your courage to have honest conversations about relationships and how a man should treat a woman kept me from being a complete "a-hole" to females (I'm sure that might be debatable). I thank you for all my life lessons about relationships and communication both intentional and unintentional.

I would also like to thank my late father, Isom W. Williams, Sr., for always supporting my various ventures and believing in me. Your presence in my life from childhood to adulthood was a true testament to how Black fathers do remain in the home and provide the needed guidance to develop the men of the future. Although you aren't here physically to see the man I've become, I pray you saw enough before you left to get a sense that you and mom did a great job. I have a good feeling if you were here, you'd say, "Damn, boy, I'm proud you." It's still tough knowing I'll never hear those words again. As with mom, I thank you for all the life lessons about marriage and communication both intention and unintentional.

To the two very best friends any man could have, I have to acknowledge my brothers Jason and Isom W. Williams, Jr. To be honest, there's nothing about the way we communicate with each other that should be in any book anywhere. It amazes me that we're even brothers and that our parents didn't just leave you both on the side of the road with a sign saying, "Free to a good home...or bad one." I appreciate all the laughs and can't thank you both enough for being there with me and for me in challenging times during childhood and adulthood. This book is born out of the resilience we developed together which influenced my vision to help other families overcome hardships as we've done.

A few other thanks are in order for my twins who give me a strong sense of purpose, inspiration, and motivation daily. Carter and Caden, because you strive to be seen, heard, and connected to in your own unique ways, you both demonstrate that even with your diagnoses of autism spectrum disorder, intellectual and developmental disability, and sensory processing disorder, effective communication both verbally and nonverbally is even more important. Thanks to the both of you, I have learned to view effective communication through a lens sensitive to abilities.

Erica, you are wise beyond your years in the communication department as a first grader. You've taught me how to improve my communication as a result of your effective, emotion-focused communication. Your ability to remind me of how my communication makes you feel and how freely you offer apologies have been a bit of a masterclass on parent-child communication. Thanks for being a great communicator and instructor.

I'd be remiss not to acknowledge my "brother from another mother" Dr. Delton DeVose. Your friendship, mentoring, encouragement, counseling, and prayers have guided me to this point in both my personal and professional life. This book would still be in draft mode inside my head if not for all the conversations we've had about family and business. I can't thank you enough for all your guidance.

To my mother-in-law, Edna Carter: Without your support during my transition out of the military, starting a therapy practice, blessing to marry Dana, relationship talks, babysitting of the kids, prayers, and so much more, I would lack the lived experiences of marriage and parenthood that influenced this book. Thank you!

I want to also acknowledge all the clients that have asked me if I have a book or when I might write a book. Well, here you go. Your trust in me with your relationship experiences have been invaluable. This book has truly been inspired by your experiences. I sincerely thank you all for your patience with this book.

Lastly, I'd like to thank True Vine Publishing Co. for all the editing, publishing, and expert guidance paired with superb professionalism. This book would truly never see the light of day without Mr. Timothy Bond and his team.

TABLE OF CONTENTS

Chapter 1

WHY "ME" CAN CAUSE MISUNDERSTANDINGS

Exploring Different Communication Styles, Needs, and Expectations in Relationships

If we look at the history of human relationships, from Adam and Eve to the present day, it becomes very clear that communication is the foundation on which positive and healthy connections are built, nurtured, and maintained. Effective communication between couples allows for the sharing of thoughts, emotions, desires, and needs, allowing for the creation and maintenance of understanding and empathy.

However, no matter how much effort we put into it, communication often remains a challenge. Despite our best efforts to convey messages clearly and with goodwill, we often find ourselves in disagreements with those closest to us. Why do these disagreements persist, even among people who deeply care for each other and respect one another? The answer lies in the individual communication styles, needs, and expectations that each person brings to the table, otherwise known as the "Me."

Communication styles are shaped by a myriad of influences ranging from upbringing and cultural background to personal experiences and temperament. They vary widely among people. Some may gravitate towards direct and assertive forms of communication, while others may lean towards a more indirect and passive approach. These differing styles can lead to misinterpretation and miscommunication, as individuals may perceive and respond to messages in ways that diverge from the sender's original intentions.

Furthermore, underlying our communication styles are a host of unspoken needs and desires that drive our interactions with our partners. These needs encompass a broad spectrum, ranging from the human yearning for connection and belonging to the more specific desires for validation, recognition, and affirmation. When these needs go unmet or are misunderstood, they can manifest as tension, resentment, or dissatisfaction within relationships.

Along with communication styles and needs, couples also bring a set of expectations that shape their interactions with their partner. These expectations, often shaped by past experiences, cultural norms, and personal values, serve as guiding principles that inform how we anticipate others to behave and respond in various situations. However, when these expectations clash with reality, they can give rise to disappointment, frustration, and conflict.

It is within this complex web of communication styles, needs, and expectations that misunderstanding and discord can pose a detrimental threat to any relationship, no matter how long that couple has been together. Despite our best efforts to communicate openly and honestly, the nuances of human interaction render us vulnerable to misalignment and misinterpretation. Yet, it is precisely through acknowledging and understanding these complexities that we can begin to navigate the complexities of human relationships with greater empathy, compassion, and resilience.

Understanding the different dynamics of communication within relationship allows us to explore strategies for fostering greater understanding, connection, and harmony within our relationships. Through reflection, dialogue, and mutual respect, we can develop communication practices that honor the unique perspectives and needs of each partner, moving from "Me" to "We" and paving the way for deeper, more meaningful connections in our personal and professional lives.

VALUES AND EXPECTATIONS

Your communication style is closely tied to your values and what you expect from yourself and from others. These learned and inherent values and expectations shape how people relate to one other. Even before we meet our life partners, our values and expectations are already a big part of us, influenced by various aspects of our lives.

Upbringing and Family. Our family and upbringing have a big impact on how we communicate. When we're kids, we learn by watching how our parents, siblings, and other relatives talk and behave, especially toward one another. These early experiences shape our basic values, like what's right or wrong, how to show love and loyalty, and what responsibilities we have.

As we grow up, the way our family communicates becomes a kind of template for our own communication style. If our family encourages open and respectful communication, we're likely to do the same. On the other hand, if our family tends to be more confrontational or avoids talking about feelings, we might pick up those habits instead. Our family also teaches us how to deal with emotions and conflicts. If our family values expressing feelings and solving problems calmly, we'll probably use those skills in our own relationships. But if our family avoids emotions or handles conflicts aggressively, we might struggle with these aspects of communication later on.

Understanding the ways that our family values and expectations prompt the development of our individual communication styles can help us be more aware of the way we speak to our partners. This then allows us to make intentional choices moving forward, ensuring that we express ourselves appropriately and effectively.

Culture and Community. Our cultural experiences also influence not just our personal identity but our sense of connection with others as well. The traditions we inherit from our communities, whether they're rooted in religious ceremonies or societal norms, contribute to a shared understanding when it comes to communication. For instance, celebrations, rituals, and customs foster a sense of togetherness, creating a bond among the people who participate in these shared practices. This shared experience helps in building a collective identity, and we start realizing that effective communication isn't just about expressing ourselves but also about understanding and respecting the diverse perspectives that make up our larger "We."

On the other hand, people who come from more individualistic societies where the collective identity is not present may lack in areas involving effective communication. This is a hurdle that will need to be worked on since the "Me" is more of a focus in individualistic cultures, rather than the collective "We."

Moving from "Me" to "We" involves a shift in focus from individual thoughts and needs to a more communal outlook. This transition is crucial for effective communication because it requires us to be mindful of our partner's backgrounds, values, and ways of expression. In a diverse community, acknowledging and embracing various cultural elements becomes essential for fostering understanding between ourselves and others. Effective communication, in this context, means recognizing the richness that different cultural perspectives bring to the table, appreciating diversity, and finding common ground for meaningful connections to thrive. It's not just about what *I* think or feel; it's about creating a space where everyone's voice is heard and valued.

Personal Experiences. Our personal experiences teach us lessons that affect not only how we view ourselves but also how we interact with others. For example, if we've faced challenges and overcome them, we might develop resilience and a more positive outlook. On the other hand, if we've encountered setbacks, we might approach situations with caution or learn to appreciate small victories more.

These experiences influence how we communicate. They shape our reactions to different situations, affecting the way we express ourselves and understand others. Positive experiences make us more open, trusting, and optimistic in our communications while challenging experiences make us more cautious, guarded, or empathetic. Recognizing the impact of personal experiences on communication helps us understand ourselves better and allows us to connect with others on a deeper level. considering the diverse backgrounds and histories that shape each person's unique communication style.

Individual Reflection and Choice. As intelligent beings with the gift of self-awareness, we can reflect on and make decisions for ourselves. In our thinking and decision-making, we continuously configure and reconfigure our values and beliefs—what really matters to us. This happens as we interact with others and when we reflect on our own thoughts and experiences.

It's crucial to know that these influences don't work alone; they mix together and shape who we are and how we see things. What we care about and expect from others isn't fixed. It changes based on our experiences and relationships. Understanding how the things we care about are shaped helps us be more understanding and caring in our relationships. This way, we build stronger connections and have more meaningful relationships with others.

COMMUNICATION STYLES

Distinguishing Effective, Ineffective, and Poor Communication

When we understand effective communication, it helps us express ourselves well and understand others better. On the flip side, recognizing ineffective communication helps us see when things aren't going smoothly, allowing us to make changes before irreparable damage is done. Even more important is being able to spot poor communication. Poor communication is a signal that something's not working right and needs to be fixed. Having an understanding of these different styles is a toolkit for better relationships, equipping you with the right way to talk *and* to listen.

Imagine communication as an arrow aimed at a target. *Effective communication* hits the bullseye with precision and accuracy, achieving its intended goal. When communication is clear, relevant, and respectful, it lands directly on target. There is no way for what is said to be misunderstood because the speaker says what they mean in a way that the listener can comprehend.

Ineffective communication misses the mark. While the arrow still lands on the board, its trajectory is erratic and uncertain. The lack of clarity, relevance, or conciseness causes it to veer off course, leading to confusion or misinterpretation. Despite reaching the board, its impact is diminished, and the intended message may not fully resonate with the recipient.

Poor communication, on the other hand, is like an arrow shot in the completely wrong direction. It not only misses the target entirely but also causes collateral damage along the way. Laden with harmful content and delivered with a destructive tone, it inflicts emotional harm and deepens rifts. Like a wayward arrow, poor communication leaves behind a trail of chaos and discord in its wake.

EFFECTIVE VS. INEFFECTIVE COMMUNICATION

When we communicate well, our message is crystal clear, leaving no room for confusion. We are telling someone exactly what we mean without any guesswork. However, it is not only clarity that is spoken with but empathy and consideration as well. In this form of communication, respect is conveyed through tone, and being polite and considerate is crucial even when we don't agree with our partner's perspective or words. This helps keep a positive environment and builds trust between people, regardless of the situation that needs navigating.

Ineffective communication, though, is like trying to connect puzzle pieces that just won't fit together. It's these ill-fitted pieces that keep people from truly understanding one another. Quite the opposite of effective communication, ineffective communication lacks clarity. This lack of clarity creates confusion, making it hard for the message to land where it's supposed to.

Effective communication is also concise—succinct and to the point, free from unnecessary verbosity or extraneous detail. Ineffective communication is filled with irrelevant information and does not focus on the essential points. We've all heard of the person who tries to "talk circles around you." These kinds of communicators tend to leave us frustrated and exhausted, which doesn't bode well for those healthy relationships we all seek to find.

This doesn't mean that you can't have long debates with your friends or family members where disagreements are bound to arise. However, when it comes to addressing concerns, conflicts, or any other issues that may impact your relationship negatively, it is critical to stay focused and to the point. How many times have you been in a disagreement and you or the person with whom you are arguing starts bringing up mistakes made years in the past? Or have you ever been in an argument with someone who cannot stop elaborating on their point, forcing you to tune out of the conversation? This happens when you lose focus of the issue at hand. By keeping the message short and sweet, we make it easy for others to understand and remember for future situations.

Effective communication goes beyond just talking; it also requires *active listening* on your part. It's not simply about hearing words but actively working to understand the other person's perspective through those words. Active listening is like turning up the volume on their thoughts and feelings, demonstrating that you're genuinely paying attention and respecting what they have to say.

When it comes to active listening, you focus not only on the words spoken but also on the emotions and intentions behind them. It's about being fully present in the conversation, putting yourself in the other person's shoes, and making a sincere effort to comprehend their viewpoint. By practicing active listening, you create a space where the other person feels valued and heard, fostering a deeper connection and making communication more meaningful. We can't just focus on what we think and feel. We also need to understand our partner's perspective, listen to their responses, and understand how they might be feeling in order to have effective, positive conversations.

When you communicate effectively, you're making things happen—whether it's sharing information, convincing someone of something, or resolving a disagreement. It's about saying what you mean in a clear way and treating the other person with respect. By speaking in a way that makes sense and by being polite, you increase the chances of reaching your goal and working together toward shared objectives.

Think of it as a successful recipe. When you mix clear words with a respectful and relevant approach, you're cooking up effective communication. It's not just about expressing yourself; it's about expressing yourself in a way that brings you and your loved one closer to shared goals. So, effective communication is more than just talking. It's about talking in a way that makes things happen and connects people.

POOR COMMUNICATION

Poor communication is like a dark cloud that hangs over our interactions and relationships, marked by significant issues that hinder healthy connections. The first sign of poor communication is the communicator who shuts down. Shutting down leaves a person in the dark without the essential information or emotional support to wade through incoming information. When communication is nonexistent or withheld, addressing issues and developing effective connections becomes impossible.

The second aspect of poor communication involves using harmful and hurtful language. This includes toxic and derogatory words, insults, or false accusations. Toxic language can vary. Not all toxic language is blatantly rude. Sometimes, it can appear as simple jesting. But even jokes have the power to negatively impact the trust in a relationship.

For example, toxic jesting could look like a man being vulnerable with his wife about a fear that she then teases him about. Even though she had no malicious intent, and even if that man laughs at the joke in good fun, he most likely will not allow himself to be vulnerable in that way again.

Another hidden toxic language is called "all-or-nothing" language. Phrases like "you always..." or "you never..." are examples of this form of speech. These toxic phrases put the other person on defense and discredits any good qualities they have all because of the one frustration at hand. This, and other kinds of damaging communication styles, have a powerful impact, shaking the foundation of trust in relationships. The recipients of such communication not only feel emotionally harmed, but they may also start questioning their own value. It's like a verbal assault that leaves scars, making individuals doubt their worth and creating a toxic atmosphere that's harmful to any relationship. In essence, when communication is filled with negativity and hurtful language, it becomes a destructive force.

Another problem that may increase the damage delivered through poor communication shows up in the way those words are delivered: with a destructive tone. This means the messages are filled with malice, contempt, or vindictiveness. It's like pouring gasoline on a fire because it intensifies the conflict. This kind of communication doesn't just stop at creating disagreements; it actively erodes trust and encourages resentment and hostility, all of which form the breeding ground for continued disagreements and destructive communication. Imagine trying to have a conversation with someone who speaks with anger and disrespect. It feels like walking on eggshells, and any hope for a healthy connection crumbles. So, when communication carries a destructive tone, it becomes a source of conflict and negativity.

Poor communication reaps vast negative consequences, causing profound harm, discord, or estrangement, that may irreparably damage relationships. When communication consistently leads to negative outcomes, it creates a toxic environment that ultimately leads to the severing of relationships.

THE CHALLENGES OF BRIDGING EXPECTATIONS AND COMMUNICATION STYLES IN RELATIONSHIPS

Navigating relationships takes a careful balance of empathy, understanding, and compromise. Unfortunately, this delicate balance can be disrupted when different communication styles and expectations collide. Personal expectations influence relationships by shaping interactions, impacting perception, influencing emotional responses, and potentially limiting growth and flexibility.

Our expectations, developed from personal and cultural values, guide us in how we engage with others.

Positive expectations can build trust, cooperation, and intimacy, enriching our connections. Conversely, negative expectations can breed mistrust and conflict, creating barriers to genuine understanding. Consider the scenario where we expect our partner to anticipate our every need. When these expectations go unmet, we tend to develop a sense of frustration or resentment which leads to a strain in our relationship. Expectations, whether positive or negative can shape the dynamics of our relationships if left uncommunicated.

Our expectations impact our perception, influencing how we perceive others' actions and words. Imagine getting a text that reads, "WHERE ARE YOU?!!" How would you perceive this communication? If you received this text from your boss during your break, you may be offended or become anxious and uncomfortable. If you received this text from your friend who you haven't seen in a year, you might jump for joy knowing that your friend must be close and is excited to see you.

The words are the same, but you perceived the tone based on your expectations of how the other person intended that communication. Recognizing that individuals are multi-faceted and influenced by various factors can foster a more nuanced understanding and approach to our relationships and our communication. We will be less apt to assume and more open to thinking out the possibilities. thus allowing us to reflect on the meaning before responding.

Our expectations can also trigger a range of emotions. The intensity of these emotional reactions is linked to the significance and rigidity of the expectation. Unrealistic or uncommunicated expectations can sow seeds of discord and resentment, undermining the emotional bond between us and our partner. Addressing these emotions requires open communication and a willingness to explore the root of the expectations, fostering a healthier emotional connection.

Fixed expectations may become barriers that stop the maturation of our relationships. Refusing to adapt or compromise can destroy relationships, especially when long-term commitments are involved. To bridge the gap between our expectations and our communication styles, we need to develop a sense of self-awareness, empathy, and effective communication skills. Openly discussing and negotiating expectations, acknowledging differences in communication styles, and committing to mutual respect and understanding can help navigate these challenges and create more fulfilling relationships.

Our expectations can serve as a type of guidance, but they are not necessarily good or bad. They should be used to help shape our interactions and perceptions within relationships, but they should not be assumed or expected when left uncommunicated. As much as we would like for our partners to just know, they cannot read our minds. It is important that we communicate expectations while also leaving room for flexibility and growth.

Self-awareness is also crucial. Navigating the impact of expectations on relationships requires self-awareness and self-reflection. Being conscious of our expectations allows us to recognize the influence our expectations may have over us and make informed adjustments when necessary.

At the end of the day, communication is fundamental to the success and longevity of any relationship, romantic or otherwise. By fostering transparent dialogue, partners can develop understanding, empathy, and collaboration, leading to stronger connections. We also need to be flexible and adapt within our relationships. These qualities are essential for fostering resilience and growth within relationships. Being able to adjust to changing circumstances and navigate challenges with grace and compassion strengthens the bond between us and our partner.

CHAPTER 2
UNDERSTANDING "MY" LOVE LANGUAGE:
APOLOGY LANGUAGES, AND COMMUNICATION STYLE

There are various aspects of our individual communication preferences that can be quantified through a series of self-assessments and quizzes. Though they may seem silly, knowing and understanding these different "languages" can actually prove to be vital when it comes to identifying our personal preferences and the preferences of our partner. Each person has a unique love language, apology language, and communication style. When you are able to communicate to your partner the ways that you prefer to receive love and apologies, they can meet your needs better than if they were to try to guess.

LOVE LANGUAGES

For those unfamiliar with the term love language, it's a concept introduced by Dr. Gary Chapman in his widely acclaimed book *The 5 Love Languages*. The idea revolves around the five ways individuals express and receive love. According to Chapman, everyone has a primary love language, a specific channel through which they feel most cherished and valued. These love languages, as outlined in the book, are broken down into 5 categories: words of affirmation, acts of service, receiving gifts, quality time, and physical touch.

When a person feels most loved through words of affirmation, they prefer to have their partner express love through positive words and compliments. Acts of service asks that love be expressed through various tasks that demonstrate your love. People who feel most loved through acts of service will value dinner being made or a clean house over compliments. Receiving gifts is about expressing love through thoughtful and meaningful presents. quality time emphasizes the importance of spending focused and undivided attention with your partner. And lastly, physical touch involves demonstrating love through physical gestures like hugs, kisses, or other forms of physical closeness.

Understanding and identifying these love languages both for yourself and your partner, can significantly improve the quality of your relationship. For a more in-depth explanation, *The 5 Love Languages* by Dr. Chapman guides readers on how to navigate and express love in a way that resonates with their partner's specific love language, fostering deeper connections and more fulfilling relationships. These languages act as a roadmap for couples to better comprehend and communicate their emotional needs while also showing their partner they love them in a way that is the most valued, ultimately enhancing the bonds that hold that relationship together.

At the core of our interpersonal connections lies the profound concept of love languages. If you are looking for a quick way to identify you and your partner's specific love language, The Love Language® Quiz can help unearth your fundamental methods of giving and receiving love.

WORDS OF AFFIRMATION

For individuals attuned to this love language, affection, appreciation, and encouragement are best expressed through heartfelt verbal affirmations. These words serve as sustenance for the soul, lifting spirits and fortifying emotional bonds.

Imagine a couple, April and John, where April's primary love language is words of affirmation. When April accomplishes a personal or professional milestone, such as receiving a promotion at work, John expresses his pride and admiration by showering her with positive words. He tells her how impressed he is with her hard work and dedication, boosting her confidence and strengthening their emotional connection. Because John knows that April feels the most loved when verbally praised, he makes it a point to shower her with verbal affection first and foremost.

QUALITY TIME

For some people, intimacy is felt most strongly through the gift of undivided attention. Shared experiences and meaningful moments lead to lifelong memories that are more cherished than material objects, allowing the giver and receiver to develop a profound sense of closeness and belonging through time spent together.

Consider a family, the Smiths, who prioritize quality time as their love language. Every Sunday, they have a tradition of spending the day together, unplugged from technology and fully engaged with each other. They might go for a hike, have a picnic in the park, or simply spend the day at home playing board games and bonding. These shared experiences create lasting memories and strengthen their family bonds.

PHYSICAL TOUCH

The language of touch is another form of emotional connection, conveying warmth, comfort, and affection in its purest form. From tender embraces to gentle caresses, physical contact serves as a potent conduit for expressing love and nurturing emotional connection for some couples.

Hernandez and Emily, a couple whose primary love language is physical touch, find solace and connection in simple acts of physical affection. A hug after a long day at work, holding hands while taking a stroll, or cuddling on the couch while watching a movie are some of the ways they express their love for each other. These physical gestures create a sense of security and intimacy in their relationship, especially in moments of crisis or anxiety where touch alleviates any negative emotions and allows the couple to become closer and provide support.

ACTS OF SERVICE

In some cases, actions may resonate louder than words, especially for those who value acts of service as their primary expression of love. Thoughtful gestures and selfless acts of kindness are valued as a demonstration care, consideration, and devotion.

Imagine a husband, Jeremy, and his wife Anna, whose primary love language is acts of service. When Anna is feeling overwhelmed with work and household chores, Jeremy takes it upon himself to lighten her load. He surprises her by doing the dishes, folding the laundry, and preparing dinner, allowing her to relax and unwind. These acts of service show his love and support, and they remind Anna that she isn't alone. She has support from her husband and can lean on him when she needs help.

RECEIVING GIFTS

The final love language shows affection through a thoughtful gift whose sentiment transcends its material value. People who value receiving gifts over the other love languages prefer to have tangible manifestations of the love shared between them and their partner. These gifts serve as a physical reminder of their person and can be cherished forever.

Jennifer, whose primary love language is receiving gifts, cherishes the thoughtful gestures of her fiancée. Because Monica is aware this is Jennifer's top love language, every Saturday morning she gets her a cup of coffee from her favorite coffee shop on her drive home from work. Even though it's not an expensive gift, Jennifer cherishes the meaning behind the cup of coffee as a small gesture that says "I see you, and I love you!"

APOLOGY LANGUAGES

Just as there are various ways to express love, there are ways in which each person prefers to receive an apology after some sort of conflict. Along with his research on love languages, Dr. Gary Chapman developed a series of what he calls apology languages. Understanding the diverse complexities that make up human communication comes down simply to these two questions: When do I, or when does my partner, feel the most loved? And how do I, or how does my partner, prefer to receive an apology?

EXPRESSING REGRET

As the most basic form of apology, some people really appreciate it when their partner says sorry in a sincere way. They want their person, who did something wrong, to admit that they messed up and genuinely feel sorry about it. In this case, a heartfelt apology is the most important when it comes to the first step of fixing things and making up.

Sam has invested a lot of time planning a romantic evening with Zoe to celebrate their three-year anniversary. Zoe comes home from work that afternoon, lays across the bed for a "quick nap", and awakens five hours later. Zoe feels devastated because she knows how much this means to Sam, and she is able to empathize with how much this hurt him. Instead of making excuses or attempting to justify her actions, she offers a heartfelt apology to Sam and validates his feelings of being hurt. Because this is his apology language, Sam is able to receive this apology and forgive Zoe rather quickly.

ACCEPTING RESPONSIBILITY

Taking ownership of mistakes and demonstrating accountability is crucial for those who identify with this apology language. They expect the person apologizing to acknowledge their role in the wrongdoing and accept responsibility for their actions. To people who value this apology language, accepting responsibility shows them that the other person actually does care about the hurt caused and that their apology is true.

Consider a situation where Kendall mistakenly double books himself one evening. On one hand, he promises to watch the kids for his wife's girl's night out, but he also promises a friend he'd help him work on his car after work. Upon getting the text message asking "Where are you?", he quickly remembers he has made a mistake. Kendall knows that accepting responsibility is Ursula's primary apology language. Instead of making excuses, Kendall takes immediate responsibility and calls stating, "Baby, I messed up and completely forgot about tonight. I remember the conversation we had but didn't put it on my calendar as I normally do. I'm headed home right now." Ursula appreciates Kendall's accountability and is better able to forgive him because Kendall has taken responsibility for his mistake.

MAKING RESTITUTION

Actions speak louder than words for individuals who value making amends and taking concrete steps to right their wrongs. They expect the person apologizing to offer to make restitution or rectify the situation in some way. This shows a sincere commitment to making things right and repairing the damage done.

Imagine a scenario where Rodney, after a long day at work and no opportunity to take a lunch break, eats his wife's leftovers from her favorite restaurant for dinner. At the very least, that could be viewed as a cardinal sin. His wife, Amy, returns home eagerly anticipating these leftovers only to discover that they are all gone. Instead of simply apologizing, Rodney takes proactive steps to make amends by having the meal that was left over delivered fresh. Amy accepts Rodney's gesture towards restitution.

GENUINELY REPENTING

For some, true repentance is the most valuable form of apology because it involves a commitment to change and a genuine desire to avoid repeating the same mistakes. Those who resonate with this apology language expect the person apologizing to express a sincere intention to learn from past mistakes and make positive changes, never allowing that same mistake to happen again. This demonstrates a willingness to grow and rebuild trust.

Let's take a look at the couple Gary and Lisa. Before going to bed one night, Lisa reminds Gary to take the kitchen trash out because she doesn't want to smell the trash in the morning. Gary agrees to do it but has forgotten for the third time in a week. Instead of the usual empty promises and relying on his memory each night, Gary acknowledges he hasn't been making the trash a priority at night and develops a plan to set a phone alarm each night at 8pm to take out the trash. Additionally, he makes it part of his routine that occurs before he watches Netflix. Consequently, Lisa is more receptive to his commitment and seeing Gary implement a change in his behavior.

REQUESTING FORGIVENESS

Another form of apology involves forgiveness. Asking for forgiveness and seeking reconciliation is essential for those who value this apology language. They expect the people apologizing to humble themselves and seek forgiveness, demonstrating humility, vulnerability, and a genuine desire to mend the relationship.

Mark makes an offhand comment about his husband James' mother after listening to him share about his strained relationship with her. Mark is aware James' primary apology language is requesting forgiveness. Instead of brushing off the incident, Mark acknowledges he was out of pocket with his comment, offers a sincere apology, and genuinely requests forgiveness. James appreciates Mark's humility and vulnerability.

COMMUNICATION STYLES

Along with the various love and apology languages, each person comes to their relationship with an already formed communication style. Understanding your specific communication style, as well as your partner's inherent forms of communication, is crucial for building and maintaining healthy relationships.

Imagine if you and your partner speak different languages; it would be challenging to convey your thoughts and feelings effectively. Similarly, everyone has a unique communication style, which translates into the way we express ourselves, listen to others, and interpret messages. By being aware of your communication style, you gain insight into how you convey information and how others perceive it. This self-awareness allows you to make adjustments, ensuring your message is clear and well-received. When it comes to your partner, it is also critical to understand their communication style in order to bypass potential misinterpretations.

There are 4 identifiable forms of communication, all of which stem from our childhood development and the experiences we have had growing up. No one is born with a set of communication styles. They develop over the course of time based on rewards or consequences received from parents, friends, teachers, employers, and previous partners. When we are able to identify the pitfalls in each style of communication, we are then able to adjust towards a more positive, healthy style that ultimately benefits our relationship in the long run.

PASSIVE COMMUNICATION

Individuals who adopt a passive communication style prioritize the needs and feelings of others over their own. They often avoid expressing their thoughts, feelings, and preferences, fearing conflict or rejection. Passive communicators may struggle to assert themselves and tend to defer to others' opinions and decisions, even when they go against their own personal wishes.

Let's take a look at Stephanie who is planning to go on a weekend getaway with her partner. Despite have a strong preference to go to a cottage in the mountains like she used to enjoy as a young girl, Stephanie remains quiet when Bobby suggests going to vacation in a large metropolitan city because she does not want to rock the boat. She goes along with the decision feeling disappointed but unwilling to voice her desires. Because of Stephanie's past experiences and childhood, she defaults to passive communication often putting the needs of others before her own. In this scenario, Stephanie clearly has a preference but chooses not to speak up because she is used to allowing others to make the decisions.

AGGRESSIVE COMMUNICATION

On the opposite end of the spectrum, aggressive communicators prioritize their own needs, wants, and feelings while disregarding those of others. They often use forceful or domineering language and behavior to assert their opinions and get their way. Aggressive communicators may resort to yelling, belittling, or intimidating others to achieve their goals, which can lead to conflict and emotional harm in relationships.

Tim has a reputation for speaking his mind as bluntly as he feels no matter who the person is. His wife, Danielle, shares she does not feel like a priority when he plays video games all day on the weekends without planning anything with her nor speaking more than a few words to her. Instead of taking accountability and addressing Danielle's thoughts and feelings in a calm and constructive manner, he deflects and yells criticisms at Danielle about her as a wife calling her selfish and entitled. In this scenario, Tim is demonstrating an aggressive communication style that creates a hostile and toxic relationship for Danielle.

PASSIVE-AGGRESSIVE COMMUNICATION

Combining elements of both passive and aggressive communication, passive-aggressive communicators express their anger or resentment indirectly. They may appear outwardly agreeable but harbor negative feelings internally, which they express through subtle or covert means. Passive-aggressive communicators often use sarcasm, backhanded compliments, or other behaviors like sulking or sabotage to convey their frustrations.

Richard is not fond of going shopping with Michelle; however, Michelle really likes spending time with him and frequently invites him to go so they can spend some quality time. Although Michelle promises to not take too much time, Richard agrees to go but frequently looks at his watch and asks how much longer the shopping will take. Furthermore, he complains Michelle is taking too much time and expresses he does not understand why it takes her so long to shop. Richard goes on to give Michelle the silent treatment as a result of his shopping experience. Consequently, Michelle feels unhappy and hurt and no longer wants to invite Richard because of his passive-aggressive communication style.

ASSERTIVE COMMUNICATION

The healthiest of the communication styles, assertive communicators strike a balance between advocating for their own needs and respecting the needs of others. They express themselves clearly, honestly, and respectfully, fostering mutual understanding and collaboration in relationships. Assertive communicators can assert their boundaries, express their thoughts and feelings openly, and engage in constructive dialogue with others.

In the vacation scenario with Stephanie and Bobby, Stephanie could respond assertively by saying, "I think the trip to a large city is one option we can put on the table, I'd like to also suggest going to a cottage in the mountains. I really need something that gets me out of the busy city life. Let's please consider this option as well." Stephanie is communicating her desires respectfully while also acknowledging Bobby's request in a manner that invites a collaborative decision-making process.

CHAPTER 3
DECODING YOUR PARTNER'S LOVE, APOLOGY, AND COMMUNICATION STYLE

In relationships, talking openly and listening well is of the utmost importance. It builds trust, pulls individuals closer, and can help lead couples through any argument. Getting to know how your partner talks and listens is key to having a happy relationship. It's time to ask yourself: Do you really know how your partner communicates?

PAY ATTENTION TO VERBAL CUES

Understanding your partner's communication style begins with paying attention to their *verbal cues*, which can offer valuable insights into their thoughts, feelings, and preferred modes of expression. Verbal cues are the actual words and phrases used when your partner talks. What they say should give you a hint at how they are feeling and what it is that they want.

For example, if someone says, "I'm really tired," they might actually mean they're upset or bored. In order to understand the true intention behind their words, we need to pay attention to the verbal cues. In this instance, we would need to look at their tone to understand that tired actually means sad. By pinpointing specific aspects of their language, such as word choice, tone and pace, and the content of their communication, we can gain a deeper understanding of how they communicate and re-late to others.

Word Choice

One of the most revealing aspects of verbal communication is word choice. Pay attention to whether your partner tends to use "I" statements or if they frequently assign blame to others. For example, if your partner says, "I feel frustrated when..." instead of "You always make me angry," it suggests a more introspective and emotionally mature communication style. Conversely, someone who habitually blames others for their feelings may struggle with taking ownership of their emotions and communicating effectively.

Moreover, consider whether your partner communicates concisely or if they prefer using metaphors and storytelling to convey their thoughts and feelings. Some individuals are naturally more succinct in their communication, while others may use vivid imagery and anecdotes to illustrate their points.

Tone and Pace

Another important aspect of verbal communication is the tone and pace with which someone speaks. Pay attention to the nuances of how your partner speaks. Is their tone calm and measured, or do they easily become agitated or defensive? Similarly, pay attention to the pace of their speech. Are they fast-paced and energetic when speaking, or do they deliberate over their words, taking pauses to reflect?

A partner who speaks in a relaxed and composed manner may feel confident and secure in their communication style, while someone who speaks rapidly and anxiously may be experiencing heightened emotions or stress. By tuning into your partner's tone and pace, you can better gauge their emotional state and respond with empathy and understanding. This understanding will help you to respond appropriately, avoiding unnecessary escalations.

Content

You should also pay attention to the actual content of your partner's communication—the topics they readily discuss and those they avoid. Do they express their needs and desires directly, or do they tend to skirt around sensitive topics? Your partner may have patterns or themes in their conversation topics and how they approach discussions about emotions, relationships, and personal experiences.

For example, if your partner is open and forthcoming about their emotions and needs, it may indicate that they feel comfortable with direct communication and value honesty and transparency in their relationships. On the other hand, if certain topics seem off-limits or they struggle to express themselves clearly, it may suggest underlying communication challenges or discomfort with vulnerability.

Paying attention to your partner's verbal cues through their word choice, tone and pace, and the content of their communication can provide valuable insights into their communication style and relational dynamics. By actively listening and observing these cues, you can develop a deeper understanding of your partners thoughts, feelings, and communication preferences, fostering greater intimacy, empathy, and connection in your relationship.

OBSERVE NONVERBAL CUES

Nonverbal communication also plays a crucial role in understanding your partner's communication style and emotional state. By observing their body language, facial expressions, and posture, you can gain valuable insights into their thoughts, feelings, and relational dynamics in a way that verbal cues may not convey. More often than not, your partner's true emotions and feelings will lie in their nonverbal cues rather than their verbal.

Body Language

One of the most revealing aspects of nonverbal communication is body language. Pay attention to how your partner's body language aligns with their verbal communication. Do they maintain eye contact, or do they avert their gaze? Are they fidgeting or displaying restless movements? Does their body appear open and relaxed or closed and guarded?

Crossed arms and an averted gaze may signal defensiveness or discomfort, suggesting that your partner may feel uneasy about the conversation. Conversely, open gestures, steady eye contact, and a relaxed posture indicates receptivity and an openness to communicate. By tuning into your partner's body language, you can better understand their emotional state and respond with empathy and sensitivity.

Facial Expressions

Facial expressions offer valuable cues about your partner's emotional state and engagement in the conversation as well. Are they smiling, frowning, or maintaining a neutral expression while engaged in conversation? Do their expressions align with the emotions conveyed through their words?

Authenticity and emotional transparency are reflected when your partner's facial expressions are congruent with their verbal communication. A genuine smile or a furrowed brow that mirrors the tone of their words indicates that your partner is expressing their true emotions. However, forced or mismatched expressions may suggest that your partner is masking their feelings or holding back from fully expressing themselves.

Posture

Your partner's posture can also provide clues about their level of engagement and comfort with the conversation. Notice whether they lean in when listening attentively or sit back when sharing their thoughts. Do they mirror your posture as a sign of rapport and connection?

A partner who leans in, maintains eye contact, and adopts an open posture demonstrates active listening and genuine interest in the conversation. On the other hand, a partner who sits back, crosses their arms, or displays closed-off body language in a hunched over manner may indicate disengagement or discomfort. By observing your partner's posture, you can gauge their level of involvement and adjust your communication approach accordingly.

ANALYZE THEIR REACTIONS IN DIFFERENT SITUATIONS

Another way that you can enhance the communication experience between you and your partner is by analyzing your partner's reactions in different situations. This may provide valuable insights into their communication style, emotional resilience, and conflict resolution strategies. By observing how they respond during disagreements, decision-making processes, and when receiving feedback, you can gain a deeper understanding of their communication tendencies and relational dynamics.

Reactions During Disagreements

One of the most revealing aspects of a partner's communication style is how they navigate conflicts or disagreements. Pay close attention to how your partner reacts when tensions arise. Do they become defensive and argumentative, seeking to assert their viewpoint at all costs? Or do they withdraw and avoid confrontation, preferring to maintain peace at the expense of addressing underlying issues? Examining how they react in the midst of an argument will lead you to better pinpointing their communication style, thus allowing you to pivot in a way that best solves the problem at hand.

If your partner becomes defensive or confrontational during disagreements, they may struggle with assertive communication and conflict resolution skills. They may find it challenging to express their feelings openly and constructively engage in dialogue with their partner. On the other hand, if your partner seeks collaborative solutions and actively listens to your perspective, they have a more adaptive approach to conflict resolution, prioritizing mutual understanding and compromise. This indicates they are able to assertively communicate, actively listen, and work together to resolve the conflict at that specific moment.

Reactions When Making Decisions

It can also be crucial to observe how your partner makes decisions as this may shed light on their communication style and relational dynamics. Pay attention to whether they value collaboration, seek input from others, or prefer to make decisions independently. Do they actively seek your input and consider your perspective, or do they make decisions unilaterally without consulting you?

A partner who values collaboration and seeks input from others demonstrates respect for differing viewpoints and a willingness to consider alternative perspectives. They recognize the importance of mutual decision-making and strive to create a sense of partnership in the relationship. This leads to healthy relational dynamics, proving that you and your partner truly can handle any situation together. Conversely, a partner who makes decisions independently or dismisses your input may struggle with communication and compromise, potentially leading to feelings of disempowerment or resentment in the relationship.

Reactions When Receiving Feedback

Another critical aspect of communication style is how your partner responds to feedback or constructive criticism. Pay attention to their reactions when receiving feedback. Do they become defensive and dismissive, seeking to justify their actions? Or do they take feedback constructively, acknowledging areas for improvement and actively working to address them?

If your partner is open to feedback and willing to learn from their mistakes, this demonstrates emotional maturity and a growth-oriented mindset. They view feedback as an opportunity for personal and relational growth, recognizing that constructive criticism can help strengthen the relationship and deepen mutual understanding. Conversely, if your partner reacts defensively or ignores feedback, they may struggle with self-awareness and accountability, hindering their ability to address underlying issues and foster open communication in the relationship.

ENGAGE IN OPEN AND HONEST CONVERSATIONS

Engaging in open and honest conversations with your partner is crucial for decoding their communication style and fostering a harmonious relationship built on mutual understanding and respect. When you are able to speak with your partner effectively, you are able to get through any disagreement in a positive manner.

Ask Direct Questions

Initiating discussions about communication preferences is key to understanding your partner's communication style. Asking direct questions such as, "What's important to you in a communication style?", or "How do you prefer to receive feedback?", and "What makes you feel heard and understood?" encourage your partner to articulate their thoughts and feelings openly.

Encourage your partner to share their perspective without judgment, and actively listen to their responses. Asking clarifying questions can deepen your understanding of their communication style and preferences, paving the way for effective communication and mutual empathy.

Share Your Preferences

You can also take the initiative to share your communication style and preferences with your partner. Express what works best for you and why. More so, openly discuss areas where your styles may differ. Not only will this communicate your needs to them, but it will also open up the door for your partner to feel comfortable in sharing their preferences as well.

By sharing your perspectives and being transparent about your needs and preferences, as well as by listening to your partner and welcoming their preferences, the routine of open communication and mutual understanding becomes easier and easier. Your willingness to be vulnerable and honest fosters trust and strengthens your emotional connection with your partner.

Actively Listen

It can also be helpful during conflict to practice active listening during conversations with your partner by giving them your full attention, maintaining eye contact, and responding empathetically. Avoid interrupting or jumping to conclusions, and strive to understand their perspective fully. Actively listening to your partner demonstrates respect and empathy, creating a safe space for them to express themselves authentically. By validating their feelings and experiences, you deepen your emotional bond and enhance your communication skills as a couple.

Be Patient and Understanding

Another form of engagement comes with the understanding that identifying your partner's communication style is a gradual process that requires time, observation, and open communication from both partners. Be patient with yourself and your partner as you navigate this journey together and celebrate the progress you make along the way.

Acknowledge that misunderstandings may occur. View them as opportunities for growth and learning in your relationship. By approaching the process with patience and understanding, you can gain valuable insights into your partner's communication style and build a stronger foundation for a harmonious and fulfilling relationship. Engaging in open and honest conversations with your partner is essential for decoding their communication style and fostering mutual understanding. By asking direct questions, sharing your preferences, actively listening, and being patient and understanding, you will form a deeper connection and navigate communication challenges with greater ease and empathy.

It is evident that decoding your partner's love language, apology language, and communication style is a fundamental aspect of fostering a deep and fulfilling relationship. Throughout our exploration of various techniques and strategies, we have emphasized the importance of understanding these unique facets of your partner's communication patterns.

By paying close attention to verbal and nonverbal cues, analyzing reactions in different situations, and engaging in open and honest conversations, you can gain valuable insights into your partner's preferences, needs, and emotional landscape. These insights serve as the cornerstone for effective communication, trust building, and

conflict resolution within your relationship. As you navigate this journey together, it is important to celebrate the
progress you make and remain patient and empathetic
towards one another. Building a deep and fulfilling relationship requires mutual respect, empathy, and a willingness to communicate openly and authentically.

CHAPTER 4:
ESTABLISHING "WE"

DEFINING SHARED VALUES, GOALS, AND VISION

When it comes to love and partnership, establishing a cohesive bond between you and your partner through shared vocabularies, values, goals, and vision can lead to a healthy, long-term relationship. Though it can be hard to combine two separate lives into one, when you take the time to discuss values and goals, you are setting your partnership up for success.

Shared values inform our actions, decisions, and behaviors, especially when it comes to our relationships. By identifying and aligning on shared values, you and your partner are better able to develop a sense of unity and cohesion that transcends individual differences and fosters a deep sense of connection. Whether it be a commitment to honesty, integrity, compassion, or adventure, shared values become the moral compass that steers the course of the relationship through the ebb and flow of life's challenges and triumphs.

Consider a couple, Jamie and Dewayne, who come from vastly different cultural backgrounds but find common ground in their shared values of kindness, empathy, and social justice. Despite their cultural differences, Jamie and Dewayne prioritize acts of kindness and compassion in their daily interactions, whether it be volunteering at a local charity or supporting each other through times of need. Their shared values bring the couple together in times of happiness and in times of strife, strengthening their bond and deepening their connection despite any barriers of culture, upbringing, and individual identity.

Once shared values are established, you and your partner will be better able to collaborate on setting common goals that reflect your collective aspirations and desires. Whether it be building a family, advancing your careers, or traveling the world, common goals provide a sense of purpose and direction, pointing you both towards a shared vision of the future. When you are in a relationship, it is no longer just you. Identifying which values you and your partner share will guide the development of your couple goals, allowing the both of you to realign during times of conflict.

Take, for example, Alex and Maya, who share a passion for environmental conservation and sustainability. Together, they set a goal of reducing their carbon footprint and living a more eco-conscious lifestyle. They commit to recycling, reducing waste, and supporting sustainable practices in their daily lives, aligning their actions with their shared values and vision for a healthier planet. Through their collective efforts, Alex and Maya not only strengthen their relationship but also contribute to a greater cause that reflects their shared values and beliefs.

Let's now imagine that Maya has a group of friends from college that she has begun to grow distant from, but this leads her to feeling like she is being a bad friend. Alex believes that these friends are not always the best influence for Maya, but Maya has a hard time letting them go. One of the biggest problems Alex has with these friends is that they like to party on the weekends, traveling to places like Vegas where they spend a ton of money on food, alcohol, and clothes. Maya doesn't like this either, but Alex knows that deciding to no longer be their friend will be difficult for Maya. So, he steers their conversation to align with their shared goal of being eco-conscious with their life. In doing this, Maya is able to clearly see that partying on the weekends and spending all of their money on material objects does not align with their shared goal, leading her to feel more confident about her decision to leave this friend group.

In addition to setting common goals, you and your partner must also envision a collective future that reflects your shared aspirations, dreams, and desires. This shared vision serves as the blueprint for decision making, guiding your actions and choices as you work together to navigate your combined life. Whether it be buying a home, starting a business, or traveling the world, a shared vision reminds the both of you that each of your decisions and successes are leading towards the pursuit of that common end goal.

Consider Sarah and Ernest, who dream of starting a family and building a home together. They envision a future filled with love, laughter, and shared memories, where they can raise children, pursue their passions, and create a supportive and nurturing environment for their family. Their shared vision serves as a source of inspiration and motivation, guiding their decisions and actions as they work towards building the life of their dreams together.

Establishing a sense of unity and cohesion within a relationship is essential to ensure that the partnership lasts. By identifying and aligning shared values, setting common goals, and envisioning a collective future, you and your partner can create a shared vocabulary that fosters mutual understanding, growth, and fulfillment.

CRAFTING A UNIFIED IDENTITY AND DIRECTION FOR THE RELATIONSHIP

Crafting a unified identity and direction for your relationship is a dynamic process that requires both individual reflection and shared exploration. At its core lies a mutual commitment to understanding and aligning values, beliefs, and aspirations. It is critical that you and your partner work through this process of self-discovery with a dual focus: both individually and together. Individually, you should take time to reflect on your core values, your individual goals, and the goals that you want to achieve within your relationship with your partner.

This process allows each of you the ability to gain clarity on your own identity and priorities, thus enabling you to have clear expectations and visions when you and your partner come together to discuss shared goals.

Simultaneously, you and your partner should engage in open and honest conversation where you both share your thoughts, revelations, and aspirations. These dialogues will invite each of you to express your individual wants and needs, making it that much easier to identify common threads and determine what your shared goals might be.

During these discussions, you and your partner should seek to identify areas of convergence and divergence in your values and aspirations. Having these conversations in an open, safe environment guarantees that common ground can be found, allowing the both of you to acknowledge the values that bind you together and the goals that you will both cherish. These conversations are also important because they will allow you as a couple to recognize and respect your differences, understanding that each of you brings unique perspectives and priorities to the relationship.

For example, Allison and Lee engage in conversations about their shared values and goals. Allison, an artist, values creativity, freedom, and self-expression, while Lee, a business executive, prioritizes stability, ambition, and financial security. Despite their differing professional backgrounds and personal interests, however, they discover common ground in their shared desire for growth, authenticity, and connection. Each partner brings something special to the relationship with their differences, but their commonalities allow them to tackle problems in a joint effort that not only strengthens them as a couple but also proves they can handle anything life throws at them together.

This collaborative effort of finding commonalities, understanding differences, and identifying strengths and weaknesses requires patience, empathy, and a willingness to compromise as you work to merge two distinct perspectives into a cohesive whole. You will work together to craft a unified identity within the relationship This doesn't mean that you both morph into the same person. It simply means that as a couple you move through life as a unit, cherishing each other's strengths and differences while also working towards that same shared goal or vision.

STRENGTHENING CONNECTION THROUGH MUTUAL UNDERSTANDING AND ALIGNMENT

Another part of developing a strong relationship involves strengthening your connection through mutual understanding and alignment by developing empathy, active listening skills, and comfort through open communication. Once you have established shared goals and values, you and your partner can begin this phase of your relationship by committing to deepening your emotional bond and fostering greater intimacy.

At the heart of this process lies *empathy*, the ability to understand and share in the feelings of another. To have a healthy, successful relationship, you and your partner should actively strive to empathize with each other's experiences, emotions, and perspectives, recognizing and validating the unique aspects of each other's inner worlds. By stepping into your partner's shoes and viewing the world through their eyes, you will be better able to connect with them and provide compassion when needed.

Imagine a scenario where one partner, Tyler, is feeling overwhelmed with work-related stress. Instead of dismissing his feelings or offering unsolicited advice, his partner, Bethany, chooses to empathize with his struggles, acknowledging the validity of his emotions and offering a listening ear. This act of empathy creates a safe space for Tyler to express himself freely, fostering a deeper sense of trust and understanding between them. This also allows Bethany to recognize when her partner feels most stressed, why he feels this way, and how she can better help him through this moment and future moments.

Active listening is another essential aspect of any healthy relationship. You and your partner should make a conscious effort to listen attentively to each other's thoughts, feelings, and needs, without judgment or interruption. This will create an environment where both of you feel heard, valued, and respected, fostering an atmosphere of mutual support and validation. Practicing this skill not only makes the act of actively listening easier and easier, but it will also allow your partner to feel that they can come to you with anything, thus ridding the relationship of any need to lie or withhold information.

Consider a scenario where Amanda openly shares her fears and insecurities with Connor. Rather than rushing to offer solutions or dismiss her concerns, Connor practices active listening, providing his full attention and offering empathetic responses when appropriate. This validation and understanding strengthens the emotional connection between them, reinforcing their bond and deepening their trust in each other. Amanda feels more sure than ever that she can go to Connor with her concerns or fears, and Connor knows that Amanda will always communicate openly and honestly with him.

When you and your partner engage in honest and transparent dialogue like the scenario above, you will be better able to express your thoughts, feelings, and desires openly and authentically. This creates a space where vulnerability is embraced, and both of you will feel safe to share your innermost thoughts and emotions. In a relationship characterized by open communication, you and your partner will feel empowered to express your needs and boundaries clearly, seeking consensus and understanding on important matters.

ALIGNING GOALS AND VISION FOR THE FUTURE

Aligning goals and developing a vision for the future is another pivotal step in the journey of building a strong and lasting relationship. With a solid foundation of connection and understanding in place, you and your partner will be able to come together to synchronize your aspirations and envision a shared path forward. This process involves setting common objectives, defining a collective vision, and reaffirming your commitment to those shared values and principles.

Setting shared goals is the first step towards aligning your trajectories. These goals may encompass various aspects of life, including personal growth, career advancement, financial stability, and relationship milestones. By identifying areas of common interest and ambition, you and your partner can synchronize your efforts and collaborate towards achieving these objectives. For example, you may set a goal to purchase a home with your partner, start a family, or start a business together. For this to be healthy and beneficial to both parties, strategic goals and visions need to be developed and implemented.

Imagine a couple, Melinda and Carol, who share a passion for travel and adventure. Together, they set a goal to visit a new country every year and immerse themselves in different cultures and experiences. By aligning their travel goals, they not only create cherished memories together, but they also deepen their bond and

Eric A. Williams, Ph.D

strengthen their connection through shared experiences and the ability to follow through on that common life goal.

In addition to setting specific goals, you and your partner must also co-create a collective vision for your future. This shared vision might include your hopes, dreams, and aspirations for yourself as an individual but also for your relationship. You should sit down and visualize the life that you both want to build together, imagining the possibilities and opportunities that lie ahead. Having a list of shared values and beliefs, shared goals, and shared life aspirations, alongside individual values and goals, is the first step in actually working towards those dreams and making them a reality.

Consider a couple, Brittany and DJ, who share a vision of creating a home filled with love, laughter, and shared experiences. They envision a future where they support each other's personal and professional growth, nurture a thriving family, and contribute positively to their community. This shared vision for their life allows them to align their couple and personal goals in a way that takes the vision from hypothetical to real.

As you and your partner align your goals and vision, you will see a drastic improvement in your commitment to those shared values and principles. Whether it be honesty, integrity, compassion, or resilience, when you and your partner pledge to uphold these values in your relationship, you will be able to achieve those goals sooner and faster than you originally believed possible.

You should begin by setting common objectives, defining what that shared path forward looks like, and reaffirming your commitment to whatever shared values you both identify as most important.

CELEBRATING ACHIEVEMENTS AND NAVIGATING CHALLENGES TOGETHER

It is also critical to recognize the importance of acknowledging and cherishing any and all milestones that you and your partner reach together. Whether it is a personal accomplishment, a professional success, or a relational milestone, you should both take pride in each other's triumphs, celebrating the victories achieved as a unified team.

Imagine a scenario where one partner, Luis, receives a promotion at work after months of hard work and dedication. Instead of solely basking in his glory, Luis' partner, Rosa, joins him in celebrating this achievement. They go out for a special dinner to commemorate the occasion, toasting Luis' success and the continued growth of their partnership. By celebrating Luis' professional milestone together, Rosa demonstrates her unwavering support and commitment to their shared journey. By doing this, Luis is able to feel even more proud of himself and proud of the support Sarah gives him which undoubtedly helped in his long-term success.

However, the journey of partnership is not without its challenges. Along the way, you will inevitably encounter obstacles and setbacks that test the resolve and strength of your relationship. This is to be expected and is completely normal. Whether navigating through financial difficulties, overcoming conflicts in your relationship, or facing external pressures, you and your partner must confront these challenges head-on and hand in hand.

Consider a scenario where Rosa, Luis, and their family face a sudden financial setback due to unforeseen circumstances. Instead of allowing this challenge to drive a wedge between them, Rosa and Luis come together to devise a solution. They communicate openly and honestly about their financial situation, brainstorming ideas, and making necessary adjustments to their budget and spending habits. Through their collective effort and mutual support, they are able to navigate through this challenging period, emerging stronger and more resilient as a couple. This proves to both of them that no matter what happens in life, if they work together, they can overcome anything.

Indeed, it is during times of adversity that the true strength of a partnership shines through. You and your partner should draw upon your shared values, mutual trust, and unwavering commitment to support each other through difficult times by offering a listening ear, a comforting embrace, and a shoulder to lean on. This provides solace and reassurance in moments of uncertainty and doubt. When this happens, you will be able to view challenges not as impossible obstacles but as opportunities for growth and learning. You'll approach adversity with resilience and optimism, recognizing that every challenge you both overcome strengthens your bond and deepens your connection.

The journey of building a strong and lasting partnership is a dynamic and multifaceted endeavor that requires dedication, effort, and mutual understanding from both partners. By establishing a sense of unity and cohesion within the relationship, you and your partner will craft a unified identity and direction, strengthen your connection through mutual understanding, and align your goals and visions for the future, paving the way for success.

As you navigate the highs and lows of life together, celebrate achievements and navigate challenges as a team. Support each other through difficult times, cherish moments of unrelenting happiness, and grow together through shared experiences.

Ultimately, building a strong and lasting partnership requires ongoing effort, patience, and dedication from both of you. By prioritizing empathy, communication, and mutual respect, you will be able to create a relationship that is built to last: a partnership grounded in love, trust, and honesty.

CHAPTER 5
CRAFTING A SHARED LANGUAGE

Communication is at the core of all human relationships. It is the medium through which emotions are shared, needs are expressed, and bonds are strengthened. Effective communication, however, is not simply a matter of exchanging words; it requires the establishment of a *shared language*, a common framework of terms, methods, norms, and boundaries that enables clear and meaningful interaction.

NEGOTIATING AND AGREEING ON COMMON TERMS AND COMMUNICATION METHODS

The first step to developing a shared language involves negotiation. As a couple, you must discuss and agree on common terms when establishing that language. This process involves open dialogue, active listening, and mutual respect as you and your partner work together to identify key terms, phrases, and expressions that hold significance for both parties. To begin this process, you may engage in reflective conversations to identify the words and phrases that resonate with the both of you. In order to accomplish this, you may need to reflect on past experiences, moments of connection, and areas of conflict to pinpoint the language that feels most authentic and meaningful to you.

Consider a couple, Sabrina and Lonnie, who are navigating a long-distance relationship. Through open and honest communication, they realize that terms like "missing you" and "thinking of you" hold significant emotional weight for both of them. They identify these terms and agree to use them as expressions of affection and longing when they are apart.

Additionally, you may need to explore communication methods that suit both of your unique needs and preferences. For this to be effective, you may need to discuss your communication styles, apology languages, and love languages to come up with the most effective array of shared terms. Not only is it critical to discuss how each of you prefer to communicate during times of difficulty, as the communication styles most often lend themselves to, but it is also important to discuss how each person in the partnership communicates during moments of joy and happiness. This will help you establish routines or rituals that promote regular and meaningful interaction.

Continuing with the example of Sabrina and Lonnie, they recognize the importance of maintaining regular communication despite the distance between them. They negotiate a communication schedule that includes daily text messages, weekly video calls, and monthly visits to ensure that they stay connected and engaged in each other's lives. As a couple, they were able to identify words and actions that are meaningful to them both, thus strengthening their trust and ability to maintain connection despite the physical distance.

Throughout the negotiation process, you and your partner must prioritize active listening skills and show one another empathy as you work to understand each other's perspectives fully. You should strive to create an environment where both parties feel heard, valued, and respected, even when discussing potentially sensitive or challenging topics. Once those common terms and communication methods have been identified and agreed upon, you can then establish clear guidelines for their use. This may involve setting boundaries around certain words or phrases to ensure that they are used respectfully and appropriately.

For instance, Sabrina and Lonnie may agree that certain terms such as "I love you" are reserved for moments of genuine affection and intimacy. They establish boundaries around the use of this phrase to prevent it from becoming diluted or insincere over time.

BUILDING CONSENSUS ON COMMUNICATION NORMS AND BOUNDARIES

Another aspect of creating a shared language comes from establishing clear guidelines for how communication should occur and identifying and respecting each other's boundaries to promote mutual respect and understanding. *Communication norms* are guidelines that you and your partner should establish for open and honest communication. You may agree to prioritize transparency and authenticity in your interactions, avoiding passive-aggressive behavior, sarcasm, or avoidance tactics during conflicts or disagreements. To counter these negative communication behaviors, you may commit to expressing your thoughts, feelings, and needs openly and respectfully, even when discussing challenging topics.

Alicia and Michael, for example, are navigating a disagreement about their household responsibilities. Instead of resorting to passive-aggressive remarks or avoiding the conversation altogether, they agree to address the issue directly and honestly. They commit to expressing their concerns and preferences openly, while also actively listening to each other's perspectives with empathy and understanding. Establishing these norms early on and re-enforcing those behaviors will make it easier and easier to naturally do them when conflicts arise in the future.

In addition to promoting open communication through an established set of norms, you and your partner may also need to discuss boundaries around certain topics or behaviors to ensure that both parties feel safe and respected within the relationship. These boundaries may include topics that are off-limits for discussion, such as past relationships or sensitive personal issues, as well as guidelines for how conflicts should be resolved.

For instance, Alicia and Michael may agree that discussions about their respective ex-partners are off-limits to prevent unnecessary tension or insecurity. They establish this boundary to protect the emotional well-being of both parties and maintain trust and respect within the relationship. Having this boundary set from the beginning will ensure that it does not cause an unnecessary argument later on in the relationship.

Furthermore, you may need to set guidelines for how conflicts should be addressed and resolved within your relationship. This may include discussing strategies for active listening, how to deliver constructive feedback and what compromises might need to be made to ensure that conflicts are approached with empathy and understanding.

Alicia and Michael may agree to use "I" statements to express their feelings and needs during conflicts, rather than resorting to blaming one another or criticizing the other's actions. They also commit to seeking solutions collaboratively and finding compromises that honor both parties' perspectives and preferences. This keeps Alicia, who is a more passive communicator, from falling into old patterns of allowing Michael to dominate any and all decisions within the relationship.

Building consensus on communication norms and setting productive boundaries requires ongoing dialogue, mutual respect, and a commitment to understanding and honoring each other's needs and preferences. By establishing clear guidelines for communication and respecting the boundaries that are set, both you and your partner are able to create a supportive and nurturing environment that promotes trust, intimacy, and growth within the relationship.

EMBRACING FLEXIBILITY AND ADAPTABILITY IN COMMUNICATION STYLES

While establishing common terms, methods, norms, and boundaries lay the foundation for effective communication, you and your partner must also recognize that communication styles may shift over time *and* in response to different situations. Recognizing the need for adjustment when discussing sensitive topics or navigating conflict is one aspect of embracing flexibility in a relationship. The needs and expectations of people are wildly complex and evolve over time; this includes you and your partner. You may find that certain topics require a more nuanced approach or a higher level of sensitivity. In these instances, it is important for both parties to be attuned to each other's emotional cues and to adjust their communication style accordingly.

Imagine a couple, Tonya and Derrick, who are discussing their financial goals. While Tonya prefers a straightforward and logical approach to the conversation, Derrick tends to become defensive when discussing money. Recognizing Derrick's sensitivity to the topic, Tonya adopts a more empathetic and supportive tone any time they navigate this topic, focusing on their shared goals and aspirations rather than placing blame or criti-

cism. This allows them to continue respecting one another while still openly and honestly communicating
about a tricky topic.

You and your partner must be willing to adapt your
communication styles as you encounter new challenges
or changes in the relationship dynamics. Relationships
are constantly evolving, and what works for communication at one stage may not be as effective at another, especially as the honeymoon phase wears off and you venture
further into a long-term, established partnership. Flexibility in communication allows you both to navigate these
changes with grace and understanding.

For instance, as Tonya and Derrick welcome their
first child, they find that their communication patterns
shift to accommodate the demands of parenthood. They
may need to adjust their communication style to prioritize efficiency and clarity amidst the chaos of caring for a
newborn, while also making time to nurture their emotional connection and support each other through the
transition. They find that while they once argued over
household finances for just the two of them, they now
feel the strain of a baby's financial burden as well. By
adapting to this life change, they are better able to communicate lovingly without adding to the stress new parenthood already brings.

In addition to adapting to changes within the relationship, you and your partner may also need to be flexible in your communication styles to accommodate differ-

ences in personality, communication preferences, and external factors. Each partner brings a unique communication style to the relationship, and being open to adapting to one other's needs fosters understanding and connection.

For example, Tonya, who is more introverted, may prefer to process her thoughts internally before engaging in discussions, while Derrick, who is more extroverted, may prefer to talk things out in real time. By recognizing and respecting each other's communication preferences, they work to find a balance that honors both their needs. They agree to address conflict in the moment when it arises, but they also agree that if Tonya needs to take a moment to process before speaking, she is allowed to take a pause, walk away, and come back to the conversation when she has gathered her thoughts.

Embracing flexibility and adaptability in communication styles is essential for creating a shared language that can withstand the complexities of a relationship. By recognizing the need for adjustment, adapting to changes in the relationship, and accommodating differences in personality and communication preferences, you and your partner will be better able to foster understanding, connection, and resilience in your communication dynamics.

Creating a shared language within a relationship is not just a task; it is a fundamental building block for fostering clear, meaningful, and respectful communication.

By negotiating and agreeing on common terms and communication methods, building consensus on communication norms and boundaries, and embracing flexibility and adaptability in communication styles, you and your partner can create a strong foundation for effective communication and mutual understanding.

Ultimately, this shared language within your relationship is not static; it should evolve and grow alongside the growth that you and your partner may see in yourselves, individually and as a collective unit.

CHAPTER 6
MASTERING THE ART OF "I" STATEMENTS

It's clear that effective communication is the cornerstone of healthy relationships. However, the way in which we as individuals articulate our needs, emotions, and concerns can profoundly influence the dynamics of our relationships and our ability to communicate effectively. *"I" statements*, a fundamental aspect of assertive communication, provide a constructive framework for expressing oneself authentically without assigning blame or accusations to others. If we can learn within our partnerships to use "I" statements, we will be better able to address conflict head on rather than assigning blame.

At the heart of effective communication lies the ability to express oneself honestly and assertively while maintaining respect and empathy for others. "I" statements offer a powerful tool for achieving this delicate balance, allowing you as the individual to take ownership of your thoughts, feelings, and experiences without resorting to defensiveness or hostility. By phrasing statements in terms of personal observations and emotions rather than attributing fault to others, "I" statements create a non-confrontational space for dialogue and understanding.

For instance, consider a scenario where one partner feels neglected by the other's busy schedule. Instead of saying, "You never make time for me," an "I" statement might be framed as, "I feel lonely and disconnected when we don't spend quality time together." By expressing your emotions in relation to how you feel rather than what they have done wrong, you are able to convey your needs and experiences without placing blame on your partner, fostering open communication and empathy.

Mastering "I" statements also involves cultivating self-awareness and emotional intelligence, allowing you to accurately identify and articulate your feelings and needs. This self-awareness enables you to communicate authentically and assertively, paving the way for deeper connection and understanding within your relationships. Moreover, by expressing vulnerability through "I" statements, you invite your partner to empathize with your experiences and offer support and validation.

In addition to fostering understanding and empathy, "I" statements play a crucial role in creating a safe and supportive environment for vulnerability within relationships. By expressing vulnerability authentically and without fear of judgment, you and your partner can strengthen your emotional bond and develop a deeper sense of intimacy and trust. In this way, "I" statements catalyze emotional intimacy and connection, allowing you to navigate challenges and conflicts with resilience and mutual support. Instead of your partner feeling like they have done something wrong or are not good enough, using an "I" statement gives them a guideline to follow in which they are able to address how you are feeling with something specific. If you say, "I feel lonely and disconnected when we don't spend quality time together," they are then able to acknowledge how you feel and respond by planning quality time for the two of you. If, on the other hand, you say, "You never make enough time for me," they may become defensive and feel as though they are working hard to provide for you but even that is not enough.

Furthermore, mastering the art of "I" statements may also involve embracing flexibility and adaptability in communication styles. While "I" statements provide a valuable framework for healthy and assertive communication, it is essential to recognize that communication styles may evolve and vary depending on the situation. By remaining open to feedback and willing to adjust your approach, both you and your partner can enhance your communication skills and strengthen your relationships.

Mastering "I" statements is essential for fostering effective communication, nurturing understanding and empathy, and creating a safe and supportive environment for vulnerability within relationships. By expressing yourself authentically and assertively through "I" statements, you and your partner can deepen your emotional connection with each other, navigate conflicts with grace and empathy, and create a relationship grounded in mutual respect and understanding.

EXPRESSING NEEDS AND EMOTIONS EFFECTIVELY WITHOUT ACCUSATORY LANGUAGE

"I" statements, also referred to as ownership statements or assertive communication, serve as a powerful tool for expressing needs and emotions effectively within relationships. Unlike *accusatory language*, which can lead to defensiveness and conflict, "I" statements encourage each person in the relationship to take ownership of their experiences and communicate in a manner that promotes openness and understanding.

Consider a common scenario in relationships where one partner feels neglected because they perceive the other partner as not listening. Instead of resorting to accusatory language, such as "You never listen to me," an "I" statement could be phrased as, "I feel unheard when I don't receive acknowledgment for my thoughts and ideas." By framing the statement in terms of personal feelings and experiences, the speaker takes ownership of their emotions and invites the listener to empathize with their perspective. This also gives the listener a direct fix that can be made rather than making them feel like they are doing something wrong.

The effectiveness of "I" statements lies in their ability to convey thoughts and feelings assertively while minimizing defensiveness and conflict. By focusing on expressing yourselves authentically without assigning blame, you and your partner create a safe space for open dialogue and mutual respect within your relationship.

Moreover, "I" statements facilitate effective communication by encouraging active listening and empathy. When you express your needs and emotions using "I" statements, you then invite your partner to listen without feeling attacked or criticized. This creates an opportunity for meaningful dialogue and understanding, as both of you can openly share your perspectives without fear of judgment.

Imagine a situation where one partner feels overwhelmed by household chores and responsibilities. Instead of saying, "You never help me with anything," they could use an "I" statement like, "I feel overwhelmed when I have to manage all the household tasks by myself." This approach allows the speaker to communicate their needs without placing blame on their partner, fostering empathy and collaboration rather than blame and resentment.

Additionally, "I" statements promote accountability and problem-solving within the relationship itself. By taking ownership of your experiences and expressing yourself assertively, you empower both yourself and your partner to address issues constructively and work towards finding solutions together. This collaborative approach will strengthen your partnership and enhances mutual respect and understanding.

"I" statements offer a constructive framework for expressing needs and emotions effectively within relationships. By focusing on personal experiences and feelings rather than assigning blame, you can create a supportive environment for open dialogue and understanding. Though it may take some practice, "I" statements will help you and your partner develop healthier communication patterns and strengthen the connection that is already there.

FOSTERING UNDERSTANDING AND EMPATHY THROUGH ASSERTIVE COMMUNICATION

Assertive communication, characterized by clear, honest, and respectful expression, is the healthiest form of communication between loving partners. This form of communication prioritizes mutual respect, active listening, and emotional validation, leading to the development of a deeper connection between each partner. "I" statements are a key component of assertive communication, encouraging each person within the relationship to express their needs and emotions in a non-confrontational manner.

When you and your partner communicate assertively by using "I" statements, you demonstrate a willingness to take ownership of your experiences and communicate your needs directly. This approach promotes understanding and empathy by creating a safe space for open dialogue and mutual respect to take place. Instead of assuming the intentions or motivations of the other person, you can focus on expressing yourself authentically while listening empathetically to your partner's perspective.

Let's look back at the scenario where one partner feels overwhelmed by household responsibilities. Rather than resorting to blame or criticism, they might use an "I" statement to express their feelings and needs: "I feel overwhelmed when I have to manage all the household chores by myself. I would appreciate your support in sharing the workload." By communicating assertively in this manner, the speaker conveys vulnerability and invites their partner to collaborate in finding a solution.

In addition to fostering understanding and empathy, assertive communication promotes healthy boundaries and mutual respect within the relationship. Couples who communicate assertively are better equipped to set boundaries effectively, expressing their limits and asserting their needs without resorting to aggression or passivity.

Moreover, assertive communication will encourage you and your partner to engage in *active listening,* a crucial component of empathy and understanding. By listening attentively to your partner's perspective and validating their feelings, you will be able to demonstrate empathy and compassion, strengthening your collective emotional bond and fostering a sense of connection.

Overall, assertive communication, facilitated by "I" statements, plays a vital role in healthy communication. By prioritizing honesty, respect, and vulnerability, you and your partner can create a supportive environment where both of your needs and emotions are heard and valued. Through the practice of assertive communication, you can develop healthier communication patterns, deepen your connection, and nurture a strong and fulfilling relationship.

CREATING A SAFE AND SUPPORTIVE ENVIRONMENT FOR VULNERABILITY

Vulnerability, often regarded as the crux of intimate relationships, requires that both people involved in a relationship feel secure and accepted enough to express their true thoughts and feelings without fear of judgment or rejection. "I" statements serve as a valuable tool in creating this safe, supportive environment as they encourage both you and your partner to share your vulnerabilities openly and authentically.

In a healthy and supportive relationship, you and your partner should show strength for each other through empathy, understanding, and reassurance, especially during challenging times. "I" statements facilitate this process by allowing you to express your emotions in a clear and non-confrontational manner, inviting your partner to show support and validation.

For instance, let's discuss a scenario where one partner is struggling with feelings of insecurity about their career prospects. Instead of bottling up their emotions or reacting defensively, they might choose to use an "I" statement to communicate their vulnerability to their significant other: "I feel anxious about my career future, and

I could use your support and encouragement during this challenging time." By expressing their feelings openly and honestly, and in a way that connects their vulnerable feelings back to themselves, the speaker creates an opportunity for their partner to offer comfort, reassurance, and assistance.

In addition, creating a safe space for vulnerability also involves active listening and empathy from both partners. When you share your vulnerabilities through "I" statements, your partner will respond with compassion, understanding, and validation. This allows both of you to demonstrate your commitment to creating a supportive environment where vulnerabilities are respected and honored.

Furthermore, creating a safe space for vulnerability requires that both you and your partner refrain from judgment, criticism, or invalidation when the other expresses their feelings. Instead, you should strive to respond with empathy, reassurance, and unconditional love. "I" statements play a vital role in creating this safe and supportive environment. By encouraging your partner to express their emotions authentically and inviting your partner's support and understanding, "I" statements can vastly improve all aspects of your relationship.

EMBRACING FLEXIBILITY AND ADAPTABILITY IN COMMUNICATION STYLES

While "I" statements provide a valuable framework for assertive communication, it's important to understand that communication styles will inevitably evolve and vary depending on the situation, context, and dynamics of the relationship. Over time, you and your partner may encounter a wide range of scenarios that require nuanced communication approaches. For example, when discussing sensitive topics such as finances, intimacy, or personal boundaries, you may need to adjust your communication style to ensure that your message is conveyed respectfully and sensitively. In these instances, employing "I" statements can help both you and your partner express your thoughts and feelings assertively while minimizing defensiveness and conflict.

Similarly, during conflicts or disagreements, you may find it beneficial to adapt your communication style to promote constructive dialogue and conflict resolution. Instead of resorting to blame or criticism, you can use "I" statements to express your perspectives and needs without placing undue pressure or responsibility on your partner. This flexible approach can direct conversations away from negative behaviors, allowing both parties the chance to communicate effectively.

As your relationship evolves and dynamics shift over time, you and your partner may need to be adaptable in your communication styles to accommodate these changes. For example, as couples navigate major life transitions such as marriage, parenthood, or career changes, they may find it necessary to adjust their communication patterns to meet the evolving needs of their partnership. By remaining flexible and responsive to these changes, you demonstrate your commitment to maintaining open, honest, and meaningful communication. When you are both willing to explore new approaches, listen actively, and respond empathetically to your partner's needs, you create opportunities for learning, compromise, and mutual growth.

While "I" statements provide a valuable framework for assertive communication, you and your partner will also need to embrace flexibility and adaptability within your inherent communication styles. Work together to determine how each of you naturally responds during conflict and in other situations, analyze the similarities and differences, and create a plan for addressing situations, both good and bad, with assertive, empathetic, and flexible communication.

Mastering the art of "I" statements is not merely a communication technique but a fundamental skill that underpins healthy and thriving relationships. By embracing this approach, you can transform the way you express yourself, how you navigate conflicts, and how you foster intimacy with your partner. Expressing your needs and emotions effectively and without accusatory language is the most important aspect of assertive communication.

"I" statements empower you to take ownership of your feelings and experiences, which leads to more assertive communication.

Ultimately, the practice of "I" statements transcends mere communication techniques; it embodies a mindset of mutual respect, empathy, and authenticity within your relationship. By mastering this art, you will watch your relationship transform

CHAPTER 7
ACTIVE LISTENING FOR UNDERSTANDING

While many may perceive communication primarily as speaking and expressing oneself, the art of active listening is equally as important. *Active listening* is a dynamic process that involves not just hearing what is said but truly understanding and empathizing with your partner's perspective. At the heart of active listening lies a profound recognition of the importance of truly hearing and understanding your partner's words, emotions, and experiences. It requires a conscious effort to set aside distractions and fully engage with what your partner is communicating. By honing your active listening skills, you can create a safe and supportive space for open dialogue, strengthen trust and empathy, and deepen your connection with your partner.

DEVELOPING SKILLS TO TRULY HEAR AND LEARN FROM YOUR PARTNER'S PERSPECTIVE

At its core, active listening is so much more than just hearing. It is about fully engaging with what your partner is saying, both verbally and nonverbally. It requires attention, focus, and a genuine desire to understand your partner's perspective.

The first step to active listening involves providing your partner with your full attention. This means listening to them without being distracted and without drifting away from the conversation subconsciously. When engaging in conversation with your partner, make a conscious effort to give them your undivided attention. Eliminate distractions such as your phone, television, or other electronic devices. Show that you are fully present and engaged by making eye contact, facing your partner, and listening without interrupting.

You can also practice using and noticing nonverbal cues. Nonverbal communication plays a significant role in conveying attentiveness and receptivity during conversations. Use nonverbal cues such as nodding your head, maintaining an open posture, and making encouraging gestures to show that you are actively listening and interested in what your partner has to say. These cues can help create a supportive and validating atmosphere for open dialogue.

While listening to your partner, make sure that you paraphrase and summarize important points made. Throughout the conversation, periodically address what your partner has said to ensure that you understand their message correctly. This not only demonstrates that you are actively listening but also allows for clarification and validation of your partner's feelings. Paraphrasing their thoughts also helps to ensure that there is no misinterpretation on your end, providing for clear and understood conversation. Reflecting on their words shows that you are genuinely engaged in the conversation and value their perspective. To accomplish this, you can also ask open-ended questions. Encourage your partner to elaborate on their thoughts and feelings by asking open-ended questions that invite deeper reflection and conversation. Instead of asking yes/no questions, pose inquiries that prompt your partner to share more openly and expansively. This demonstrates your interest in their perspective and encourages them to express themselves fully.

The last component of active listening involves the validation of their feelings. Acknowledge and validate your partner's feelings, even if you don't necessarily agree with their perspective. Let them know that their emotions are valid and worthy of acknowledgment. You can use the phrase, "I understand that you are feeling…" By acknowledging their feelings, you create a supportive and validating environment where your partner feels heard and understood.

By incorporating these strategies into your communication with your partner, you can develop the skill of active listening which deepens your understanding of their perspective.

PRACTICING EMPATHETIC LISTENING AND REFLECTIVE RESPONSES

Practicing empathetic listening and offering reflective responses is another essential component of effective communication and the building of emotional intimacy in relationships. Empathetic listening means that while you're hearing your partner speak, you are working to understand their perspective and put yourself in their shoes.

Listen without judgment. Create a safe and nonjudgmental space for your partner to express themselves freely. Avoid interrupting or criticizing their thoughts and feelings. Instead, listen with an open mind and heart. Show empathy and understanding, even if you don't necessarily agree with their perspective. In doing so, you'll be better able to put yourself in their shoes. Empathetic listening involves stepping into your partner's shoes and viewing the situation from their perspective. Try to imagine how they might be feeling and what their experiences might be like. This empathetic perspective-taking can help you better understand their emotions and respond with love.

You can also spend time reflecting on their feelings. Think back on your partner's feelings and experiences to show that you understand and empathize with their perspective. Use phrases like, "It sounds like you're feeling frustrated because..." or "I can see why you would feel anxious about..." This reflective approach validates your partner's emotions and demonstrates that you are genuinely listening and are engaged in the conversation.

Once they have communicated how they feel, offer support and encouragement. Express empathy and offer support to your partner by validating their feelings and encouraging them to continue being open and honest. Let them know that you are there for them and are willing to support them through whatever challenges they may be facing, whether those challenges are about you or are about your partner's individual life. Reassure them that their emotions are valid and worthy of acknowledgment while also offering words of encouragement to help them feel understood and supported.

By practicing empathetic listening and offering reflective responses, you can foster a supportive and understanding relationship dynamic where both partners feel heard, valued, and respected. This promotes emotional intimacy and strengthens the foundation of the relationship, allowing you to navigate challenges and joys together with empathy and compassion.

DEEPER CONNECTION THROUGH MUTUAL UNDERSTANDING

When we actively listen to our partners with empathy, we also deepen the connection because we are showing a want for mutual understanding between ourselves and our partner. By mastering the art of active listening for understanding, you and your partner can create a relationship grounded in trust, empathy, and respect.

The first, and oftentimes most difficult, way to deepen the connection with your partner by allowing them to better understand you is by sharing *your* perspective as well. Mutual understanding is a two-way street. While it is important to listen to your partner's perspective, it is equally important to share your thoughts, feelings, and experiences openly and honestly. Though it is

important to listen to your partner when they are expressing their concerns or frustrations, it is equally as important for you to tell them how you are feeling in that moment as well.

You can also work towards practicing patience.
When listening to your partner's perspective, be patient
and empathetic as they articulate their thoughts. Avoid
rushing to judgment or trying to "fix" their problems. Instead, focus on truly understanding their point of view
and empathizing with their emotions. Validate their feelings and experiences, even if they differ from your own.
Through this, it will be easier to honor each other's differences and find common ground when working to resolve those differences. Recognize and celebrate the fact
that you and your partner may have different perspectives, experiences, and ways of thinking. Rather than
viewing these differences as obstacles, see them as opportunities for growth and learning within the relationship. Embrace diversity and appreciate the unique qualities that each partner brings to the table.

Those differences will also allow you to collaborate
on solutions. When faced with challenges or conflicts,
approach them as a team. Work together with your partner to find solutions that honor both your needs and preferences, utilizing each person's individual strengths to
guide that process. Focus on finding win-win outcomes
that strengthen your connection and deepen your understanding of each other.

And finally, practice gratitude and appreciation. Show them that you are thankful for your partner's willingness to share their perspective and engage in open communication. Let them know that you value their thoughts, feelings, and experiences, and that you are committed to continuing the hard work that comes with navigating the ups and downs of a relationship. Celebrate the moments of connection and growth that you experience together, too. When a positive outcome is reached, or when you notice your partner change their communication style to create a safer atmosphere, praise their flexibility and willingness to grow with you.

Mastering the art of active listening for understanding is not a skill that should be taken lightly. Active listening will enable you and your partner to create a safe and supportive space where thoughts, feelings, and experiences can be freely shared and understood. It fosters empathy, trust, and respect.

CHAPTER 8
EXPRESSING LOVE IN YOUR SHARED LANGUAGE

At the heart of any relationship lies the endeavor to discover unique ways to convey your love, to show your partner that you value their preferences and desires in big and small ways. Just as every individual possesses a distinct love language, so too does each partnership harbor its lexicon of affectionate gestures and expressions. For some, love may manifest through words of affirmation spoken tenderly in moments of vulnerability and joy. For others, love may be found in acts of service, in the small, everyday deeds that speak volumes of devotion and care.

Though the acknowledgement of love languages is critical in any relationship, meaningful actions and behaviors are another aspect that need to be discovered and utilized. Intimacy may be best expressed via soft touch and the warmth of a lengthy hug. From great romantic gestures to tiny acts of kindness, each action strengthens the link between lovers. Consider the husband who surprises his wife with breakfast in bed on a dull Sunday morning or the partner who puts love notes throughout the house as a reminder of their passion. These seemingly insignificant actions often build on top of one another, reminding you and your partner that love can be shown in all ways. It is in the rhythm of daily life that love finds its most enduring expression. From a tender kiss goodbye in the morning to a heartfelt "I love you" whispered before drifting off to sleep, these seemingly mundane gestures carry profound significance, anchoring partners in a shared language of love and belonging. It is through these daily rituals of connection that partners reaffirm their commitment to each other.

The art of expressing love in your shared language is a multifaceted journey, one that requires patience, understanding, and a willingness to embrace vulnerability. It is a journey of discovery, exploration, and growth, where you and your partner learn to communicate your love in ways that resonate deeply with each other's hearts. By nurturing this shared language of love, you and your partner can create a relationship that is rich in intimacy, connection, and unwavering devotion.

DISCOVERING UNIQUE WAYS TO EXPRESS LOVE AND APPRECIATION ALIGNED WITH YOUR PARTNER'S PREFERENCES

Understanding and aligning with your partner's love language is akin to unlocking the door to their heart's most cherished desires. Each individual possesses a unique lexicon of love, a personal dialect that speaks volumes about their deepest emotional needs and desires. Whether it is through words of affirmation, acts of service, receiving gifts, quality time, or physical touch, discovering and embracing your partner's love language is a transformative journey that fosters intimacy, connection, and emotional fulfillment within the relationship.

Consider the case of Rachel and Bryce, a couple navigating the maze of expressing love within their relationship. Rachel, a woman of depth and introspection, finds solace and affirmation in quality time spent together. For her, meaningful conversations and shared experiences are the currency of love that binds their hearts together. On the other hand, Bryce, a man of action and devotion, feels most loved when Rachel expresses her affection through physical touch and acts of service. For him, the warmth of her embrace and the thoughtfulness of her deeds speak volumes of her love and devotion.

In recognizing and honoring each other's love languages, Rachel and Bryce are better able to understand one another and reciprocate affection. Rachel carves out dedicated time for heartfelt conversations and intimate date nights, cherishing each moment spent in Bryce's presence. She listens attentively to his words, offering words of affirmation and encouragement that uplift his spirit and affirm his worth. In turn, Bryce showers her with thoughtful gestures, such as preparing her favorite meal or running errands to ease her burden, demonstrating his love and devotion in action. Through their commitment to honoring each other's love languages, Rachel and Bryce's relationship is able to withstand any challenge.

Discovering unique ways to express love and appreciation aligned with your partner's preferences is a transformative journey of self-discovery and mutual understanding. It requires patience, empathy, and a willingness to step outside of oneself to truly see and appreciate the essence of your partner's being. By embracing each other's love languages, couples can create a relationship that is rich in intimacy, connection, and emotional fulfillment—a testament to the enduring power of love in all its forms.

CULTIVATING INTIMACY THROUGH THOUGHTFUL GESTURES AND ACTIONS

Another aspect of healthy relationships involves intimacy through attentiveness and devotion, where thoughtful gestures and actions allow partners to show their love all the time. Not every couple is able to incorporate grand romantic gestures into their everyday life. Showing love consistently through small actions can hold even more weight if utilized correctly.

Consider the tale of Minnie and Jasper, a couple who have mastered the art of nurturing intimacy through thoughtful actions. Minnie, with her keen eye for detail and deep understanding of Jasper's preferences, delights him with surprise love letters tucked under his pillow or small tokens of appreciation that speak directly to his heart. These seemingly minor gestures carry profound significance, conveying Minnie's love and affection in ways that resonate deeply with Jasper's soul.

In return, Jasper, fueled by his desire to express his love for Minnie in meaningful ways, orchestrates romantic dinners under the stars or plans spontaneous adventures to reignite the spark in their relationship. His efforts to create moments of magic and wonder for Minnie demonstrate his unwavering commitment to nurturing their bond and keeping the flames of passion alive.

As Minnie and Jasper exchange these gestures of love and devotion, they lay the foundation for a relationship characterized by intimacy, trust, and mutual understanding. Each thoughtful action serves as a building block in the construction of their shared connection.

Beyond grand romantic gestures, intimacy also involves the daily expression of love and affection in the small moments shared between partners. It is in the gentle touch of a hand, the lingering gaze across a crowded room, or the spontaneous laughter shared over a private joke. These seemingly mundane interactions carry immense significance.

Moreover, building relationships through thoughtful gestures and actions extends beyond romantic occasions or special events; it is a way of life, small choices made every day to show affection. It is in the simple act of making breakfast in bed on a lazy Sunday morning or surprising your partner with their favorite dessert after a long day at work. These small acts of kindness and thoughtfulness demonstrate your love and appreciation for your partner in tangible ways, strengthening the intimate connection shared between you. This shows that you are attuned to your partner's needs, desires, and preferences, and making a conscious effort to express your love in ways that resonate deeply with them.

As Minnie and Jasper have discovered, showing intimacy everyday is a deeply rewarding one, filled with moments of joy, laughter, and shared experiences. They are able to celebrate the unique connection shared between them and nurturing it with care and devotion, day by day, moment by moment. In addition, as they continue to exchange gestures of love and affection, they reaffirm their commitment to each other and lay the groundwork for a relationship that will stand the test of time.

NURTURING CONNECTION THROUGH DAILY EXPRESSIONS OF AFFECTION

Nurturing a deep and enduring connection within a relationship requires more than just grand gestures and occasional displays of affection as it demands a commitment to expressing love and appreciation in the everyday moments shared between partners. Amid life's chaos, it's these daily expressions of affection that serve as the glue that holds a relationship together, fostering intimacy, trust, and emotional closeness.

Take, for example, the story of Jasmine and David, a couple who understand the importance of nurturing connection through daily expressions of affection. For them, love is not just something to be celebrated on special occasions. It is woven into the fabric of their daily lives, expressed in countless small but meaningful ways.

Their day begins with a simple yet profound ritual: a tender embrace and whispered declarations of love exchanged as they greet each other in the morning. This intimate moment sets the tone for the day ahead, infusing their interactions with warmth and tenderness from the very start.

Throughout the day, Jasmine and David find numerous opportunities to express their love and appreciation for each other. Whether it is a heartfelt text message sent during a busy workday, a spontaneous phone call just to say, "I miss you," or a lovingly prepared meal shared in the evening, their gestures of affection serve as constant reminders of the deep bond they share.

Even amid life's challenges and responsibilities, Jasmine and David make time for each other, carving out moments of connection amidst the chaos. They steal glances and share smiles across crowded rooms, find solace in each other's presence during moments of stress or uncertainty, and offer words of encouragement and support when needed most. Perhaps most importantly, Jasmine and David never underestimate the power of physical touch in nurturing their connection. Whether it is a lingering hug, a gentle caress of the hand, or a spontaneous kiss planted on the cheek, these simple acts of affection speak volumes of their love and devotion to each other.

In the evening, as they unwind from the day's activities and prepare for rest, Jasmine and David take time to reflect on the moments they have shared. They express gratitude for the love and support they have received from each other and reaffirm their commitment to nurturing their relationship for years to come. Through their daily expressions of affection, Jasmine and David have created a relationship that is characterized by warmth, tenderness, and emotional intimacy. Their commitment to nurturing connection in the small moments of everyday life has strengthened their bond and deepened their love for each other in ways they never thought possible.

Nurturing connection through daily expressions of affection is about prioritizing love in all its forms and recognizing the profound impact that small gestures can have on a relationship. It is about making a conscious effort to show appreciation for your partner, even amid life's hectic schedules and distractions and creating a space where love can flourish and grow, day by day, moment by moment.

Expressing love in your shared language is indeed a sacred dance as well as an intimate interplay that binds two hearts together. By taking the time to understand and honor your partner's love language, you demonstrate a profound level of care and commitment to your relationship. Whether it is through acts of service, words of affirmation, quality time, physical touch, or receiving gifts, aligning with your partner's preferences creates a deep sense of connection and intimacy that transcends words alone.

CHAPTER 9
NAVIGATING CONFLICT CONSTRUCTIVELY

Conflict is an inevitable part in any relationship. However, it is not the presence of conflict that defines the relationship, but rather how we navigate and resolve these conflicts that determine the strength and resilience of our bond. Conflict, when approached constructively, can be a catalyst for growth, understanding, and deeper connection between partners. It is a natural part of any relationship, arising from differences in perspectives, needs, and expectations. Rather than avoiding conflict or allowing it to escalate into destructive patterns, you and your partner can learn to navigate disagreements in a way that fosters understanding and mutual respect. This begins with the recognition that conflict is not inherently negative. In healthy relationships, it is an opportunity for growth and deeper connection.

Shared communication tools play a crucial role in resolving conflicts respectfully and collaboratively. These tools include active listening, "I" statements, time-outs, and setting ground rules for communication. Active listening involves fully engaging with your partner's perspective, demonstrating empathy, and seeking to understand their point of view without judgment or interruption. "I" statements allow individuals to express their feelings and needs assertively, without resorting to blame or criticism. Timeouts provide a respectful pause in the conversation to cool off and collect thoughts while setting ground rules ensures that communication remains respectful and productive.

Implementing strategies for effective problem-solving and compromise is essential for resolving conflicts constructively. It helps with identifying the root cause of the conflict, brainstorming potential solutions, and being willing to compromise to reach a mutually beneficial outcome. Flexibility, creativity, and a willingness to consider alternative perspectives are key to successful problem-solving. Seeking mediation from a neutral third party can also help resolve particularly challenging conflicts.

Ultimately, navigating conflict constructively strengthens the relationship through resolution and growth. Conflict resolution is not about winning or losing but about finding common ground and moving forward together. Cultivating empathy, fostering forgiveness, learning from mistakes, and celebrating progress are all important aspects of the conflict resolution process. By approaching conflict with openness, empathy, and a commitment to growth, partners can deepen their understanding of each other, strengthen their bond, and emerge from conflicts with a stronger and more resilient relationship.

USING SHARED COMMUNICATION TOOLS TO RESOLVE DISAGREEMENTS RESPECTFULLY AND COLLABORATIVELY

In every relationship, conflict is inevitable. How we choose to handle these conflicts can either strengthen our bond or create further discord. Effective communication is the key to resolving disagreements constructively and maintaining a healthy relationship. There are many different ways that you, individually, and with your partner can develop the skills necessary for communicating effectively when conflict does arise.

Active Listening

Active listening is a fundamental aspect of effective communication, especially during conflicts. It involves fully engaging with your partner's perspective, both verbally and nonverbally. While actively listening, it is critical to give your partner your full attention. When your partner is expressing their thoughts or feelings, make a conscious effort to give them your undivided attention. Put away distractions such as your phone or computer, maintain eye contact, and avoid interrupting. You can also paraphrase what they have already said and reflect on what it means and how it makes you feel. Throughout the conversation, periodically rephrase or reflect on what your partner has said to ensure that you understand their perspective correctly. This demonstrates that you are actively listening and encourages your partner to continue sharing. You may also need to acknowledge and validate your partner's feelings, even if you do not necessarily agree with their viewpoint. Let them know that you understand how they feel and that their emotions are valid and worthy of acknowledgment.

"I" Statements

"I" statements are a powerful communication tool that allows individuals to express their needs and concerns without placing blame or accusing their partner. By taking ownership of your feelings and using non-confrontational language, you create a safe space for open dialogue. When using "I" statements, express your feelings openly and honestly. Start your statements with "I feel" to express your emotions without making accusations. For example, instead of saying, "You never listen to me," you could say, "I feel unheard when I don't receive acknowledgment for my thoughts and ideas." Utilizing these statements will help you remain focused on yourself, on how you feel. Keep the focus on your own experiences and emotions rather than blaming or criticizing your partner. This helps to avoid defensiveness and encourages your partner to listen with an open mind.

Speak calmly and assertively, avoiding aggressive or accusatory language that can escalate the conflict. Be mindful of your tone and body language to ensure that your message is received in a non-threatening manner. During the conflict, if you feel that emotions are running high, making it challenging to communicate effectively, then it could be most effective to take a timeout from the conversation. Agreeing to take a timeout can provide both you and your partner with an opportunity to cool off and collect their thoughts before continuing the discussion. Agree on a set of ground rules for using timeouts, including how long they will last and where each partner will go to cool off. This helps to prevent misunderstandings and ensures that timeouts are used constructively. If you are feeling negative emotions, you may want to use the timeout period to engage in self-soothing activities such as deep breathing, going for a walk, or practicing mindfulness meditation. This can help to reduce stress and restore emotional balance. It is also critical to determine how long the timeout will last and stick to it. This prevents the issue from being swept under the rug and ensures that both partners have an opportunity to address it when they are calmer and more rational.

While in the midst of conflict, establishing ground rules for communication can ensure that you both maintain a respectful and constructive tone. Ground rules provide a framework for productive dialogue and help to ensure that conflicts are resolved fairly and respectfully.

The most important ground rule is to avoid personal attacks. Refrain from using hurtful or disrespectful language during conflicts. Instead, focus on expressing your thoughts and feelings calmly and respectfully. Keep your tone of voice calm and respectful, even if you feel upset or frustrated. Avoid raising your voice or using aggressive language that can escalate the conflict. Allow each partner to express their thoughts and feelings without interruption. This ensures that both perspectives are heard and respected. And finally, practice active listening by listening to your partner's perspective without interrupting or criticizing them. Avoid making assumptions or jumping to conclusions, and instead, focus on understanding their point of view.

Effective communication is essential for resolving conflicts constructively and maintaining a healthy relationship. By utilizing shared communication tools such as active listening, "I" statements, timeouts, and setting ground rules, you and your partner will be able to navigate disagreements more respectfully and collaboratively. These tools promote understanding, empathy, and ultimately, stronger relationships in the long run.

IMPLEMENTING STRATEGIES FOR EFFECTIVE PROBLEM-SOLVING AND COMPROMISE

Once communication tools are in place, the next step is to implement strategies for effective problem-solving and compromise. Conflict resolution is a vital skill in any relationship, requiring both you and your partner to work together to find mutually acceptable solutions.

Identify the Root Cause

The first step to resolving conflict is by identifying the underlying issues contributing to the disagreement. Often, conflicts arise from deeper-rooted issues such as unmet needs, unresolved emotions, or differing values. By addressing the root cause of the conflict, you can work towards finding lasting solutions that promote understanding and reconciliation.

Start by engaging in open and honest dialogue with your partner. Encourage them to share their perspective and actively listen to their concerns without judgment. Reflect on your feelings and motivations and be willing to acknowledge any role you may have played in the conflict. Once you have a better understanding of the underlying issues, focus on finding common ground and exploring potential solutions that address the root cause of the conflict. Remember that the goal is not to assign blame but to work together toward resolution and reconciliation.

Brainstorm Solutions

Effective problem-solving involves generating multiple options and considering alternative approaches. Set aside time to sit down with your partner and brainstorm potential solutions to the conflict. Create a supportive environment where both partners feel comfortable sharing their thoughts and ideas. Encourage creativity and open-mindedness during the brainstorming process. Consider all options, no matter how unconventional they may seem, and be willing to explore different approaches to resolving the conflict. Avoid dismissing ideas prematurely and keep an open mind to new possibilities.

Once you have generated a list of potential solutions, evaluate each option carefully, considering the potential benefits and drawbacks. Look for solutions that address the underlying issues while also respecting the needs and preferences of both partners.

Practice Flexibility

Flexibility is another essential aspect when seeking to resolve conflicts and reach a compromise. Be willing to adjust your expectations or preferences to find solutions that meet the needs of both you and your partner to the greatest extent possible. Remember that compromise does not mean sacrificing your values or principles but rather finding common ground and seeking mutually acceptable solutions.

Approach the conflict with a mindset of collaboration rather than competition. Focus on finding win-win solutions that benefit both parties and strengthen the relationship. Be open to feedback from your partner and willing to consider alternative viewpoints.

It is also important to recognize that flexibility extends beyond the specific issue at hand. Conflict resolution often requires a willingness to adapt and grow as individuals and as a couple. Embrace opportunities for personal and relational growth, and approach conflicts as opportunities for learning and development.

Seek Mediation if Necessary

In some cases, conflicts may be too difficult to resolve on your own, especially if emotions are running high or communication has broken down. In such situations, seeking mediation from a neutral third party can be beneficial.

Consider reaching out to a therapist, counselor, or trusted friend or family member to serve as a mediator. A mediator can provide an unbiased perspective, facilitate productive communication, and help you find common ground. They can also offer guidance and support as you work towards resolution. Be open to the guidance and insights offered by the mediator, and approach the mediation process with a willingness to listen and compromise. Remember that seeking mediation is not a sign of weakness but rather a proactive step toward resolving conflicts constructively and respectfully.

STRENGTHENING THE RELATIONSHIP THROUGH CONFLICT RESOLUTION AND GROWTH

While conflicts may initially strain your relationship, they also present opportunities for growth. By approaching conflicts with a mindset of learning and growth, you and your partner can emerge from challenging situations with a deeper understanding of each other and a stronger bond.

Develop Empathy

Empathy is the most vital emotion necessary for a healthy relationship, especially during times of conflict. Practice empathy by putting yourself in your partner's shoes and seeking to understand their perspective. Recognize that you and your partner may have valid feelings and concerns, even if they differ from your own.

For instance, imagine yourself in your partner's position, experiencing the situation from their perspective. Visualize how they might be feeling and what their underlying needs and motivations might be. By empathizing with your partner, you create a sense of connection and mutual understanding that fosters trust and compassion.

Take Ben and Mary, for example. Mary is a schoolteacher who spends most of her days working with over 100 kids. When she comes home, she is exhausted. Ben, on the other hand, works remote and is more flexible with his career. Mary becomes frustrated because she often comes home and is expected to then make dinner and take care of her and Ben's 2-year-old. If Ben placed himself in Mary's shoes, he might better understand why this has frustrated her. He then, might also work to help her when she gets home.

Foster Forgiveness

Forgiveness is essential for moving past conflicts and rebuilding trust. Holding onto resentment and grudges only perpetuates negative feelings and hinders the healing process. Instead, practice forgiveness by letting go of past grievances and focusing on moving forward together with a renewed sense of commitment and understanding.

For example, picture forgiveness as a bridge that spans the gap between you and your partner, allowing you to cross over from hurt and resentment to healing and reconciliation. As you release the burden of anger and resentment, you pave the way for greater closeness and connection in your relationship.

Let's take a look back at Ben and Mary. Instead of getting mad or yelling at Ben for not helping her, Mary is able to forgive him for his lack of help. Because of this forgiveness, they are able to come together and create a plan that allows both adults to feel heard and helped, rather than resorting to passive aggressive arguments.

Learn from Mistakes

Conflicts offer valuable opportunities for learning and growth. Instead of viewing them as setbacks, see them as opportunities to reflect on what went wrong and how you can approach similar situations differently in the future. Use conflicts as a catalyst for personal and relational growth, embracing the lessons they offer. Imagine conflicts as steppingstones on the path to a stronger and more resilient relationship. With each conflict you navigate and overcome, you gain valuable insights and skills that contribute to your growth as individuals and as a couple. Embrace the opportunity to learn and evolve together.

Celebrate Progress

Acknowledge and celebrate the progress you make as a couple in resolving conflicts and strengthening your relationship. Recognize the effort and commitment it takes to navigate conflicts constructively and celebrate each step forward together.

For instance, you can visualize your relationship as a garden that requires nurturing and care to flourish. Each conflict you successfully navigate is like a flower blooming in the garden, symbolizing growth, resilience, and renewal. Take the time to celebrate your achievements and milestones, both big and small, as you continue to thrive in a more resilient relationship.

Over their 5 years of marriage, Kendrick and Angela have always argued over whose job it is to take the trash out. What started out as a small annoyance grew into something much more. Angela notices that every other week she takes out the trash, but the other times Kendrick does it. She decides that this is a good system and prepares a nice dinner for Kendrick to thank him for his help and to celebrate their progress at both taking the trash out on alternating weeks.

Build Resilience

Conflict resolution builds resilience within the relationship by demonstrating the couple's ability to overcome challenges together. Every conflict successfully navigated strengthens the bond between partners, enhancing their ability to weather future storms.

To illustrate this, think of conflict resolution as a workout for your relationship muscles. Just as physical exercise strengthens your body, navigating conflicts strengthens your relationship. Each conflict overcome builds resilience and fortitude, empowering you and your partner to face future challenges with confidence and unity.

Deepen Connection

Conflict resolution provides opportunities for deeper connection and intimacy between partners as well. By engaging in open and honest communication during conflicts, you and your partner gain insight into each other's thoughts, feelings, and perspectives, fostering a deeper emotional connection.

By cultivating empathy, fostering forgiveness, learning from mistakes, celebrating progress, building resilience, and deepening connection, couples can strengthen their relationship through conflict resolution and growth. Conflict, when approached constructively, can catalyze positive change, leading to greater understanding, intimacy, and resilience within the relationship. Embrace conflicts as opportunities for growth and transformation, and watch as your relationship flourishes and thrives in the face of adversity.

Navigating conflict constructively is an essential skill for building a healthy and resilient relationship. By using shared communication tools to resolve disagreements respectfully and collaboratively, implementing strategies for effective problem-solving and compromise, and embracing conflict as an opportunity for growth and strengthening, you and your partner can navigate conflicts with grace and resilience.

Conflict resolution is not about avoiding disagreements altogether but rather about approaching them in a way that fosters understanding, respect, and growth. When conflicts arise, couples who communicate openly, listen empathetically, and work together to find solutions can emerge from challenging situations with a deeper appreciation for each other and a stronger bond.

APPENDIX

Below is a list of various communication exercises and activities for you and your partner to practice developing your shared language.

Daily check ins. Establish a routine where you and your partner check in with each other daily. This could be during breakfast, before bed, or any other convenient time. Share your highs and lows of the day, express gratitude for each other, and discuss any concerns or challenges you are facing. This regular practice fosters open communication and strengthens your connection.

Reflective listening. Practice reflective listening by taking turns sharing your thoughts and feelings while the other partner listens without interruption. After one partner speaks, the listener paraphrases what they heard to ensure understanding before responding. This exercise promotes empathy and deepens understanding between partners.

Relationship vision board. Create a vision board together that represents your shared goals, values, and aspirations as a couple. Use images, words, and phrases to visualize your ideal relationship and the life you want to build together. Discuss each element and how you can support each other in achieving these goals. This activity strengthens your bond and reinforces your commitment to each other's happiness and fulfillment.

Role-playing scenarios. Role-play common communication scenarios, such as discussing finances, making major decisions, or resolving conflicts. Take turns playing different roles and practice using your shared communication tools in realistic situations. This helps you become more comfortable with expressing yourselves and finding constructive solutions together.

Appreciation jar. Start an appreciation jar where you both write down things you appreciate about each other on small pieces of paper and add them to the jar regularly. Set aside time to read from the jar together during moments of tension or disconnect. This simple yet powerful exercise reminds you of the positive aspects of your relationship and reinforces gratitude and love.

BOOKS

1. *The Seven Principles for Making Marriage Work* by John Gottman

- Description: This book offers valuable insights into building a strong and lasting marriage based on extensive research conducted by renowned relationship expert John Gottman. Gottman outlines seven principles that are essential for maintaining a healthy relationship, providing practical advice and exercises for couples to implement in their own lives.

- Key Topics: Communication, conflict resolution, intimacy, trust, emotional connection

- Target Audience: Married couples, couples in committed relationships, relationship counselors

2. *Nonviolent Communication: A Language of Life* by Marshall B. Rosenberg

- Description: Marshall B. Rosenberg introduces the concept of nonviolent communication (NVC) as a powerful tool for fostering understanding, empathy, and connection in relationships. Drawing on his experience as a mediator and psychologist, Rosenberg offers practical guidance on expressing needs, resolving conflicts, and cultivating compassionate communication.

- Key Topics: Empathy, emotional intelligence, conflict resolution, self-awareness, effective communication

- Target Audience: Individuals seeking to improve their communication skills, couples in conflict, therapists, educators

3. Hold Me Tight: Seven Conversations for a Lifetime of Love by Dr. Sue Johnson

- Description: Dr. Sue Johnson presents a transformative approach to strengthening relationships through emotional connection and attachment. Based on her groundbreaking work in Emotionally Focused Therapy (EFT), Johnson outlines seven conversations that couples can engage in to deepen their bond and foster intimacy that lasts a lifetime.
- Key Topics: Attachment theory, emotional bonding, relationship dynamics, healing past wounds, creating a secure connection
- Target Audience: Couples seeking to enhance their emotional connection, therapists, marriage counselors

4. The Five Love Languages: The Secret to Love that Lasts by Gary Chapman

- Description: Gary Chapman introduces the concept of love languages as a framework for understanding how individuals give and receive love. By identifying their primary love language, couples can enhance communication, strengthen emotional bonds, and develop deeper intimacy in their relationships.

- Key Topics: Love languages, communication styles, expressing affection, relationship satisfaction, emotional connection
- Target Audience: Couples, individuals seeking to understand their own and their partner's emotional needs, therapists, relationship coaches

5. *Getting the Love You Want: A Guide for Couples* by Harville Hendrix

- Description: Harville Hendrix explores the concept of "Imago," the unconscious image of love that influences our relationships. Through practical exercises and insights, couples can learn to heal past wounds, break destructive patterns, and create a more fulfilling and harmonious partnership.
- Key Topics: Healing childhood wounds, conscious relationships, communication skills, mutual growth, rekindling passion
- Target Audience: Couples seeking to improve their relationship, therapists, marriage educators

6. *Attached: The New Science of Adult Attachment and How It Can Help You Find – and Keep – Love* by Amir Levine and Rachel Heller

- Description: Amir Levine and Rachel Heller delve into the science of adult attachment styles and how they impact romantic relationships. By understanding their attachment styles, individuals can navigate dating, communication, and intimacy more effectively, leading to healthier and more fulfilling connections.

- Key Topics: Attachment theory, relationship dynamics, emotional needs, communication patterns, forming secure bonds
- Target Audience: Singles navigating the dating scene, couples seeking to understand relationship dynamics, therapists, counselors

WEBSITES

1. The Gottman Institute (https://www.gottman.com/)

• Description: The Gottman Institute offers a wealth of resources, articles, and online courses based on the research of Drs. John and Julie Gottman. Visitors can access valuable insights and tools to enhance communication, manage conflict, and build lasting relationships.

• Key Features: Relationship quizzes, blog posts, workshops, webinars, and access to certified Gottman therapists

• Target Audience: Couples, individuals seeking relationship advice, therapists, educators

2. Psychology Today's Relationship Center (https://www.psychologytoday.com/us/therapy-types/relationship-issues)

• Description: Psychology Today's Relationship Center provides a comprehensive collection of articles, expert insights, and therapist directories focused on various aspects of relationships. Visitors can explore topics such as communication, intimacy, and conflict resolution to gain valuable guidance and support.

• Key Features: Articles, expert blogs, therapist directory, forums, and discussion boards

• Target Audience: Individuals seeking relationship advice, couples in need of support, therapists, researchers

3. The Couples Institute (https://www.couplesinstitute.com/)

• Description: The Couples Institute offers a range of resources and programs designed to help couples navigate challenges and strengthen their relationships Founded by renowned therapists Ellyn Bader and Peter Pearson, the institute provides online courses, workshops, and therapy services tailored to couples' needs.

• Key Features: Online courses, workshops, articles, therapy services, and expert advice

• Target Audience: Couples seeking relationship support, therapists specializing in couples therapy, relationship educators

4. Marriage.com (https://www.marriage.com/)

• Description: Marriage.com is a comprehensive platform that provides resources and support for couples at every stage of their relationship journey. Visitors can access articles, advice columns, and expert insights covering topics such as communication, intimacy, and conflict resolution.

• Key Features: Articles, expert advice, relationship quizzes, online therapy services, and community forums

• Target Audience: Couples seeking relationship guidance, therapists specializing in couples counseling, marriage educators

5. The Relationship School (https://www.relationshipschool.com/)

• Description: The Relationship School offers online courses, workshops, and coaching programs designed to help individuals and couples create healthy and fulfilling relationships. Founded by relationship expert Jayson Gaddis, the school provides practical tools and strategies for improving communication, resolving conflicts, and deepening intimacy.

• Key Features: Online courses, coaching programs, podcast episodes, articles, and community support

• Target Audience: Individuals and couples seeking relationship skills training, therapists, and relationship coaches

6. LoveLearnings (https://www.lovelearnings.com/)

• Description: LoveLearnings is a valuable resource for individuals and couples seeking practical advice and insights on love, dating, and relationships. The website features articles, quizzes, and expert tips covering a wide range of topics, from building trust to navigating long-distance relationships.

• Key Features: Articles, relationship quizzes, expert advice columns, product reviews, and downloadable resources

- Target Audience: Singles looking for dating advice, couples seeking relationship guidance, therapists, relationship educators

7. BetterHelp Relationship Advice (https://www.betterhelp.com/advice/relationships/)

- Description: BetterHelp offers a dedicated section on relationship advice, featuring articles, videos, and expert insights aimed at helping individuals and couples navigate the complexities of modern relationships. Visitors can access practical tips and resources to improve communication, resolve conflicts, and strengthen emotional connections.
- Key Features: Articles, videos, expert advice, online therapy services, and community support
- Target Audience: Individuals and couples seeking relationship advice and support, therapists, counselors

8. 5 Love Languages: https://5lovelanguages.com/quizzes/love-language

THERAPISTS

1.   Psychology Today Therapist Directory: Psychology Today offers a comprehensive therapist directory where you can search for licensed marriage and family therapists (LMFTs) or couples counselors in your area. The directory allows you to filter your search based on location, specialties, therapeutic approaches, and accepted insurance plans, making it easy to find a therapist who meets your specific needs and preferences.

2.   GoodTherapy.org: GoodTherapy.org is another valuable resource for finding licensed marriage and family therapists (LMFTs) and couples counselors in your area. The directory provides detailed profiles of therapists, including their areas of expertise, therapeutic approaches, and client reviews. You can search for therapists based on location and specialties, ensuring you find the right fit for your relationship goals.

3.   Gottman Method Couples Therapy: Consider seeking out therapists who specialize in Gottman Method Couples Therapy, an evidence-based approach developed by Drs. John and Julie Gottman. This approach focuses on enhancing couples' friendship, intimacy, and conflict-resolution skills through structured interventions and exercises. Therapists trained in Gottman Method Couples Therapy can help you strengthen your relationship and improve communication patterns.

4.   Emotionally Focused Therapy (EFT) for Couples: Another effective approach to consider is Emotionally Focused Therapy (EFT) for Couples, which helps couples identify and change negative interaction patterns and strengthen emotional bonds. EFT therapists work with couples to explore underlying emotions and attachment needs, facilitating healing and deeper connection. Look for therapists trained in EFT who can guide you through the process of rebuilding trust and intimacy in your relationship.

5.   American Association for Marriage and Family Therapy (AAMFT): The American Association for Marriage and Family Therapy (AAMFT) website offers a directory of licensed marriage and family therapists (LMFTs) who adhere to the highest professional and ethical standards. You can search for therapists by location and specialties, including couples therapy, and verify their credentials to ensure you are working with a qualified professional.

6.   National Registry of Marriage Friendly Therapists: The National Registry of Marriage Friendly Therapists is a database of therapists who are committed to helping couples strengthen their relationships and avoid unnecessary divorce. You can search for therapists by location and view their profiles to learn more about their approach to couples therapy and areas of expertise.

7. **TherapyTribe**: TherapyTribe is an online directory of therapists, counselors, and mental health professionals offering a range of services, including couples therapy. You can search for therapists by location, specialties, and therapeutic approaches, making it easy to find a qualified professional who can support you and your partner on your journey to a healthier relationship.

www.ingramcontent.com/pod-product-compliance
Lightning Source LLC
Chambersburg PA
CBHW060240030426
42335CB00014B/1552